A[MW00427181

Walking with Francis of Assisi

"I have great respect for Dr. Bruce Epperly and, like millions of others, profound love for St. Francis. What a gift to have his reflections on this great saint whose example is needed now more than ever!
—BRIAN D. MCLAREN, author of *Faith After Doubt*

"A beautifully written account of a theologian's spiritual journey with the beloved saint. Each chapter moves us, step-by-step, a little closer to the heart of Francis, while offering a transforming vision of mystical activism for our time."
—PATRICIA ADAMS FARMER, author of *Beauty and Process Theology*

"Discover the face of Christ on this word-journey through Assisi with Bruce Epperly. He traverses the landscape, shares snapshots of his childhood in dialogue with the life and spiritual development of St. Francis, and offers spiritual practices that call us to greater reflection and activism."
—REV. DR. CHARLENE ZUILL, Spiritual Life Coordinator, Boston University School of Theology

"Details of St. Francis's teaching and exemplary life are compellingly and creatively integrated with personal reflections from the author's own spiritual journey, along with offering contemplative practices to ground one's own social justice work. The energy to continue working for environmental justice is grounded in the spiritual exercises he shares with the reader."
—JAY TERBUSH, Pilgrimage Guide and Intentional Interim Minister, United Church of Christ

Walking with Francis of Assisi

From Privilege to Activism

BRUCE EPPERLY

franciscan
media®
Cincinnati, Ohio

LIBRARY OF CONGRESS CATALOGING-IN-PUBLICATION DATA
Names: Epperly, Bruce Gordon, author.
Title: Walking with Francis of Assisi : from privilege to activism / Bruce Epperly.
Description: Cincinnati, Ohio : Franciscan Media, [2021] I Summary: "From a pilgrimage through the streets of Assisi to contemplative walks on the beaches near his home, Bruce Epperly has pondered the questions of privilege, prayer, and social justice while walking with the teachings of Francis of Assisi"-- Provided by publisher.
Identifiers: LCCN 2020038925 (print) I LCCN 2020038926 (ebook) I ISBN 9781632533319 (paperback) I ISBN 9781632533326 (ebook)
Subjects: LCSH: Francis, of Assisi, Saint, 1182-1226. I Francis, of Assisi, Saint, 1182-1226--Influence. I Christian saints--Italy--Assisi--Biography. I Social justice--Religious aspects--Christianity. I Walking--Religious aspects--Christianity. I Christian pilgrims and pilgrimages. I Christian life--United Church of Christ authors.
Classification: LCC BX4700.F6 E67 2021 (print) I LCC BX4700.F6 (ebook) I DDC 271/.302--dc23
LC record available at https://lccn.loc.gov/2020038925
LC ebook record available at https://lccn.loc.gov/2020038926

Cover and book design by Mark Sullivan
Copyright ©2021, Bruce Epperly. All rights reserved.
ISBN 978-1-63253-331-9

Published by Franciscan Media
28 W. Liberty St.
Cincinnati, OH 45202
www.FranciscanMedia.org

Printed in the United States of America.
Printed on acid-free paper.
21 22 23 24 25 5 4 3 2 1

CONTENTS

Franciscan spirituality is inspired by gratitude for the graceful interdependence of life. As I write these words, self-sequestered in a time of pandemic, I am filled with truly heartfelt gratitude for the gift of life, for the beauty of the earth, and for those persons who have shaped my life.

This book is the gift of synchronicity. Although Francis is one of my spiritual mentors, I never intended to write a book about the significance of Franciscan spirituality for twenty-first century people. But, in the amazing and gentle providence of life, new paths open, awakening us to new adventures in faith and creativity. In mid-September 2019, I received an anxious appeal from the religion editor of our local paper, the *Cape Cod Times*, telling me that the person scheduled to write the "Faith and Values" piece for early October was unable to complete the assignment, and asking if I would fill in for him. I had enough to do as a village pastor, who regularly takes care of my two young grandsons, and I was also in process completing another text for publication. As I always do when an unexpected request comes my way, I went to the beach to ask for God's guidance as I opened my senses to the beauty of Nantucket Sound. I quickly received the spiritual guidance I needed, "Go ahead, and you will have the inspiration and creativity necessary. Writing this article will be a gift to others and it may change your life, too." Given the upcoming Feast of St. Francis, held on October 4, I decided to write a short piece on Francis as a mystical activist. By chance—or was it by providence?—the president of Franciscan Media saw the piece posted online and reached out to me. Once again, I took the invitation to the beach, prayerfully considering whether another Francis text was needed and if I was the person to write it. Within an hour of walking, the answer came and with it a proposed outline to send to the publisher!

I am grateful for Kelly McCracken and Alicia von Stamwitz for their belief that this book can make a difference in the challenges of twenty-first century living. I am grateful to my ministerial colleague Jay Terbush for the invitation to be a co-leader of a pilgrimage to Assisi. I am grateful to three wise women who read this text and provided comments: my classmate from James Lick High School, now fifty years ago, Cheryl Cementina; my student and now colleague in ministry, Cyndi Simpson; and my personal and intellectual friend, Patricia Adams Farmer. I am thankful for my congregation, South Congregational Church, United Church of Christ, Centerville, Massachusetts. In the spirit of *ubuntu*, "I am because of you," I give thanks for my family, my two grandsons and their parents, and my companion of over forty years, Kate. In the spirit of the Navajo spiritual guides, I affirm "with beauty all around me, I walk." I received many of my insights as well as the go-ahead to write this book on morning walks on Craigville and Covell's beaches. May we delight in this good earth, loving our Mother and caring for all her creatures.

—*Bruce Epperly*
Cape Cod, Massachusetts

Saintliness for Our Time

I hope your encounter with this book is as timely as my writing of it. At this moment, my family and I are self-sequestered between our homes and the nearby Cape Cod beaches and trails. Perhaps, at my moment of writing, you are hunkered down in your own home, praying for a planetary and local healing from COVID-19. I believe that Francis's message is even more important in light of this most recent pandemic. Francis—and his spiritual sister, Clare—remind us we are all connected. The paths of greed, consumerism, individualism, and nationalism endanger the planet and its peoples. In the spirit of Francis, we need to break down barriers of friend and stranger, citizen and immigrant, rich and poor, if we are to survive in this increasingly interdependent world. Nations need to see patriotism in terms of world loyalty as well as self-affirmation. We need the Franciscan vision of all creation singing praises to the Creator if we are to flourish in the years and centuries to come. Like Francis and Clare, we need to become earth-loving saints, committed to our planet and its peoples—in our time and our children's and grandchildren's time.

A Protestant Journeys with Francis

L ike many people, my first encounter with Francis involved a
bird feeder. As a young child, tagging along with my mother
on a visit to a friend, I spied the statue of a strange-looking man,
with an equally strange haircut—one that resembled Moe's from
the Three Stooges!—in the backyard. "Who's that?" I asked my
mom. She responded, "That's St. Francis, the patron saint of
birds and beasts." At the time, the only saint I knew about was
St. Nicholas, known to me as Santa Claus. We Baptists had little
knowledge and even less appreciation for the long tradition of
saints and mystics in Christian history. For us, Jesus and the Bible
were the direct path to God the Father. We didn't need Catholic
saints or Mother Mary to be our intermediaries when we could
go right to Jesus.

In those pre-Vatican II days, Protestants and Catholics were
equally suspicious of one another and equally ignorant of the
riches of each other's traditions. I recall an incident from my
childhood in King City, California, a small town in Salinas Valley,
the heart of Steinbeck country. One Friday afternoon, my friend
Richard Pozzi and I were sauntering home from baseball practice. As we passed the local Baptist church where my dad was
pastor, I asked Richard if he wanted to come in. He responded, "I
wish I could. But Catholics aren't supposed to go into Protestant

churches. I think it might be a mortal sin." We didn't even know what a mortal sin really meant, but we were told that we could be friends on the ball field but not at church. There was a spiritual boundary we couldn't cross if we were to remain faithful to our own faith traditions. Growing up in the Baptist church, I can't recall hearing anything meaningful about Ash Wednesday, Lent, saints, or the seasons of the Christian year until I reached college!

The boundaries of my childhood had become a thing of the past as I sought to be global in my faith and spirituality. Over the years, Francis had become one of my mentors. Although the mechanics of Francis's sainthood and the canonization process were unimportant to me, his spirit had inspired and enlightened me and provided an important complement to the theological and spiritual gifts of the progressive Protestant tradition with which I now identified—free-spirited, congregational, Bible-centered, prayerful, and joining contemplation and social activism. I thought Francis might have appreciated the open-spirited social commitment of the progressive Christian movement in which I located myself. I knew that although eight hundred years separated us, Francis and his spiritual companion Clare, or Chiara, had much to teach me about how to navigate the maelstrom of twenty-first century life. Rooted in their own time, they were also spiritual contemporaries for our own time and our quest to choose life in a death-filled world.

CHAPTER ONE

Francis: A Saint for Our Time

Most High,
Glorious God,
enlighten the darkness of my heart,
and give me
true faith,
certain hope,
and perfect charity,
sense and knowledge,
Lord,
that I may carry out
Your holy and true command.

(Francis, "A Prayer before the Crucifix")[1]

The first day of my pilgrimage to Assisi was dawning and I wanted to get the lay of the land and reorient my spiritual GPS after three hectic days of sightseeing in Rome. No one stirred, not even a stray cat or dog in search of bounty from a trash can, as I passed the majestic Basilica di San Francesco, the church of Santa Maria Maggiore, the abbey of San Pietro, and the Basilica di Santa Chiara. Too early even for morning mass, I walked the cobblestones and heard sounds of a new day dawning. As I gazed at the verdant Umbrian countryside in the distance, my imagination went back to a simpler time. I visualized the hilltop village eight centuries ago, without lights or power, phones or internet, insular and isolated, a place where most of its citizens lived and died without traveling more than day's walk from their Umbrian birthplace.

In the still, crisp morning, I experienced the simplicity of a time before climate change, global travel, the novel coronavirus, and the 24/7 news cycle. For a split second, I forgot the machinations of political leaders and the spirit of unrest that has enveloped the globe as I pondered the journey of another pilgrim like myself, trying to make sense of his own inner stirrings and the challenges of his own time and place and looking for a way of life that would nurture his spirit and serve the world. I was looking for a world-affirming way to become a mystic activist for our time.

Eight centuries ago, young Giovanni di Pietro di Bernardone, called Francesco (the Frenchman) because of his father's love of France and later for his stylish apparel, may have walked down the same street, today's Via San Francesco, returning from a nocturnal dalliance, tipsy and wobbling a bit, weary and ready for a few hours of sleep as the rest of the town prepared for work. By all accounts, young Francesco was a generous and free spirit, with a ready smile and an open wallet. When the workday was over, he often caroused with companions, courted beautiful women, and feasted on the best cuisine Assisi had to offer.

But there was a hidden side to him, unknown to his companions, that might have guided his footsteps in the predawn hours. Could this popular and generous youth have wakened before sunrise looking for a quiet place to pray, training his eyes for a sign alerting him to a new and very different adventure? Could he have been imagining something more than affluence, materialism, and power? Could God have been whispering beneath his festive songs, inviting him to deeper joy and purpose for his life?

Augustine of Hippo, the North African bishop and theologian, speaks of our restless hearts finding peace only when we encounter the Living God. Perhaps awakened by a quiet but urgent voice, what the apostle Paul describes as the Spirit's "sighs too deep for words," the young man who was to become St. Francis paused a few minutes for contemplative prayer, looking for direction from a God he did not yet know.

I can visualize Francesco gazing at sunrise over the Umbrian valley below Assisi, eyes fixed on the horizon and captivated by the dilapidated chapel of San Damiano less than a mile outside the city walls. For all his privileges—financial security, status in the community, the expectation of a beautiful wife, and the hope of knighthood—that insistent, still, small voice may have whispered, "there is more, yes, there is more to life than financial success and social standing. There is a greater beauty even than the loveliest maiden of Assisi." In his quest for upward mobility and status, Francesco had planned to align himself with a regional nobleman. Deep down he may have experienced an unnamed spiritual uneasiness: What if there was a higher cause and a greater leader to whom he should give his allegiance? An inner voice queried, "Why serve the servant when you can serve the Master?" But who was the Master and what would the Master require?

It Will Be Found in the Walking

I am a walker. Indeed, walking is one of my favorite pastimes. I rejoice in sunrise while striding on the beach near my home or through urban landscapes when I'm traveling on business.

I delight in an afternoon saunter with my wife, Kate, and our goldendoodle, taking in the beauty of Cape Cod as my dog gallops across the beach. Knowing my love for walking, a dear friend once gave me a glass paperweight, inscribed with Augustine's words: *solvitur ambulando*, "it will be solved in the walking." Movement awakens novel visions and stimulates creative thinking. It's difficult to hold onto old ideas when you're on the move. Walking becomes the place of possibility, intimacy, and service. God is our companion as we venture toward new horizons.

In my own predawn peregrination on Assisi's ancient byways, I was looking for a spiritual home. My search was for spiritual calm but also to find a launching point for further spiritual adventures as a writer, pastor, professor, and contemplative activist. Anxious about my grandchildren's future in a world where climate catastrophes are becoming the new normal and incivility and bullying run rampant, I was in search of a quiet center to inspire creative process and political involvement.

In the middle of my morning reverie, I realized that although I could not physically go back in time, I could invite Francis to be a contemporary, a fellow seeker after truth, beauty, and justice. I could imagine a twenty-first century Francis walking beside me pointing out the spiritual landscape of his time and sharing his wisdom for responding to the spiritual challenges of mine. Every adventure is unique, but each spiritual journey involves a vision and restlessness, a quest for horizons stretching beyond social expectations, political alignments, and even religious expectations. Francis discovered that, despite being a military prisoner recovering from the trauma of battle, the everyday world whose values he took for granted was not his only option. His life could be different. The world could be a very different place than he had imagined. It dawned on him that his destiny might involve becoming one of God's messengers, midwifing in time and space the Reality that beckoned him. He realized he had the freedom to become a citizen of a world not yet born, living by a different set of values than his parents and peers, and inviting them to see life from a new perspective: God's vision rather thirteenth-century consumerism, parochialism, and status-seeking.

Francis was on the edge of an adventure in spiritual transformation that would take him from privilege to prayer and from self-interest to world loyalty. His journey would inspire future adventurers to follow the path of spiritual activism, imagining a transformed church responding to a transformed world. Though a person of his time, using the theological categories and spiritual practices available to him, he transformed these categories in a way that enabled him to become a spiritual guide for all seasons.

Taking a New Path

Many people seek certainty in the religious life. Familiar words and doctrines suffice. Well-traveled pathways provide enough adventure for their journeys. Others are drawn forward by doubts, questions, and spiritual restlessness. God, apple pie, and the flag are not enough to quench their spiritual thirsts. Institutional religion has let them down, giving them stone instead of bread or defining their deepest loves as illicit. Political and religious platitudes celebrating past certainties cannot provide the bread of life that will satisfy their spiritual hungers.

In the wake of his release from prison after an ill-fated military excursion, Francis, like many of today's spiritual seekers, began to ask questions about God's presence in the world, and what God wanted from him. Was following God limited to the confines of good citizenship and obedience to religious and civil authorities? Or was encountering God the catalyst for spiritual adventure and prophetic critique? Did citizenship in God's realm require him to jettison social standing and economic security? Was God a companion or competitor? Intimate or stranger? In those moments of convalescence and recovery, perhaps young Francesco, the good-natured man about town, asked "Does God have a vision for my life? If so, how will I discover it?"

Faithful Iconoclasm

Francis's spiritual quest is mirrored in our quests for deeper and more abundant lives. These adventures are almost always iconoclastic and put us at odds with the values of our immediate culture and the world around us. At various times of my life, I remember hearing that inner voice of God and asking questions that led me as a pre-teen to take the first steps in leaving the Baptist church of my roots. The fundamentalist faith, with its clear boundaries of saved and unsaved and right and wrong, was too small, too binary, for my emerging spirit. The God of my childhood was too cramped to encompass my queries about the scope of salvation and the eternal destiny of other religious traditions. I finally made my break from my childhood church in high school to embark on the magical mystery tour of the late 1960s, wandering with Bilbo and Gandalf, opening the doors of perception to other dimensions through psychedelics, learning to meditate, and then, to my surprise, returning to a free-spirited Baptist church where questions were welcomed and a young man's gifts were affirmed. In letting go of the familiar and domesticated faith and expectations of my childhood, I was Franciscan in spirit without knowing it!

Four decades after my teenage and college transformations, I still had questions as I followed in the footsteps of the *Poverello*, the "Little Poor One of Assisi." Questions had lured me to take this pilgrimage to Assisi. Not only questions related to the lectures I would be giving to my fellow pilgrims in Assisi but questions about my own vocation and service. At retirement age, but still professionally active, healthy, and vital, I felt a new stirring. Aware of my mortality, I pondered what, in the words of Mary Oliver, I would do with my "one wild and precious life." My physical journey reflected my inner spiritual adventures as a pastor, professor, writer, husband, grandparent, father, and friend. Francis's life challenged me to look beyond the narrow circle of self-interest to embrace a vision of world loyalty that would encompass my family and the nation but expand to include the whole earth. I needed to translate my love for my grandchildren into care for vulnerable, starving, and imprisoned children across the globe and in my own nation. I needed to chart a way of life that would promote planetary healing for generations to come.

I pondered God's call to Francis, "rebuild my church," and realized that as a pastor, parent, and professor, I too am responsible for playing my part, however insignificant, in rebuilding the church and revitalizing an earth-healing faith for my time. More than that I came to realize that the parish of every follower of Jesus today is not only their local community but the whole earth in its tragic beauty and wonderful brokenness. What would I do in the next few decades, should I live that long, to bring beauty and healing to the earth? How would I as a spiritual leader challenge the forces of incivility, chaos, hatred, and exclusion, while yet seeing something of God in those whose viewpoints and political policies I oppose?

In my mid-sixties, I also felt in the words of Francis the tug of Brother Ass, or Brother Body, in my daily life. I love the physical world, but I recognize its limits in terms of aging, temptation, and habitual behaviors. I knew that I must forge a positive relationship with embodiment to support my hopes for vital and meaningful aging and come to terms with my eventual death.

With Francis, I was confronted with the realities of violence, not merely the violence of a holy war, the twelfth- and thirteenth-century crusades sponsored by spiritual leaders, but the violence of chaotic national leadership, bullying and bloviating political messages, the collusion of church and state, and the polarization splitting families and communities and threatening the social fabric of national life. Despite my commitment to healing the earth through my personal and political efforts, the pilgrimage to Assisi was a much-needed respite from NPR, CNN, and PBS, and the constant online news feeds. I needed to journey inward to build the foundation of the outward journey of faithful discipleship and ministry. I needed to reach out to the marginalized and forgotten from a quiet and energetic spiritual center. It was important for me to find the right balance between restlessness and peace, prophetic critique and conciliatory healing. On my predawn peregrinations through Assisi, I found myself walking the paths of Francis, as he had sought to walk the paths of Jesus, knowing that life's deepest questions are found in the walking.

As I walked the streets of Assisi, I realized I needed the wisdom of this saint who sought to reform the church based on his experience of the Living God. I recognized that the church always needs reformation, but this reformation needs to be grounded in inner spiritual experience and not just external institutional change. I sought a faith that honored but went beyond denominational labels to help me find common cause with others who are seeking to heal the earth, regardless of faith tradition or spiritual experience.

Continuing Reformation

At the heart of the Protestant Reformation that emerged some three centuries after Francis's time was the affirmation that the reformed church is always reforming. Following God's way creates a spiritual restlessness, a sense that God always has more in store for us than we ask or imagine. While he was loyal to the church of his birth, Francis felt this divine restlessness as he entered the church of San Damiano to pray. Gazing at the Crucified One, Francis heard the voice of a God that he did not fully know whispering, "Rebuild my church." Being a concrete thinker, Francis initially assumed that God had called him to rebuild this dilapidated church and other neglected churches nearby. Only later did it dawn on Francis that God had called him to be a companion in rebuilding and reforming the church of his time. Like the apostle Paul, who counseled, "do not be conformed to this world, but be transformed by the renewing of your minds" (Romans 12:2), Francis came to recognize that the inner journey of spiritual transfiguration was wedded to the outer journey of social and ecclesiastical transformation.

New visions of God inspire new behaviors and expand our circle of concern. Missional commitments and acts of compassion deepen our spirits and remind us, in the spirit of today's creation spirituality, that "God is all things and all things are in God." Francis's mystical activism transcended the binary categories of tradition and innovation, doctrine and experience, flesh and spirit, human and nonhuman, God and the world, and propelled his quest to be God's companion in healing the earth and its creatures. Today, we need this same agile spirit to confront individually and institutionally the critical challenges of our world.

Saintly Synchronicity

Francis lived in a God-filled world. For the pilgrim of Assisi, the heavens declare the glory of God—and so do sparrows, wolves, and worms. Our cells and souls reflect divine wisdom and are constantly being energized and replenished, even inspired by God. In a God-saturated world, synchronous events populate our days, if our spirits and senses are open. Around each corner is a burning bush or a ladder of angels for pilgrims of the sprit. But, more than that, God wants us to move from mysticism to activism, midwifing and giving birth to God's vision in our personal lives and public responsibilities. Synchronicities abound for those who live prayerfully, asking for guidance and then listening to God's wisdom moving through their lives.

Francis believed in divine synchronicity and saw it as essential in the spiritual adventure. Surely it was synchronous that Francis showed up at the church of San Damiano and then listened to the guidance he received. No doubt it was synchronous for Francis to notice a leper as he traveled the roads of Umbria. Mortified and disgusted by leprosy, Francis may have wished to pass by on the other side of the road. But God's still, small voice told him to stop, reach out, and embrace the man with leprosy. Both the man with leprosy and Francis were transformed in that moment. But, when Francis looked back as he continued the journey, the man with leprosy had disappeared. Francis wondered if the man was Christ in disguise; as he embraced the leper, was he embracing Jesus?

Saints and mystics train their senses to be open to God's presence. In my spiritual companionship with Francis, walking on Assisi roads and Cape Cod beaches, I have made a commitment to see God in all things and all things in God. I have exclaimed with Francis and his followers, "My God and all things." I felt God's call to pay attention to intuitions, insights, dreams, and encounters, knowing that I may be entertaining angels without knowing it (see Hebrews 13:2).

I am not alone in my journey to experience God in my personal life and citizenship. I suspect that you are on a journey of mystical activism, too. I invite you to consider making a commitment to look for divine messages everywhere. Listen to your life, and out of that listening, let your life speak in acts of transforming love.

A Saint and Mystical Activist for Our Time

Sainthood can be a blessing and a curse. Dorothy Day, social activist, spiritual guide, and one of the founders of the Catholic Worker Movement, protested against those who admired her generous and saintly spirit: "Don't call me a saint. I don't want to be dismissed that easily."[2] Day recognized that saints could be categorized as so heavenly minded that they are perceived to be no earthly good! Untouched by domestic life, saints can be discarded as irrelevant to the challenges most of us face daily: raising a family, working, and political involvement. Beneath her protestation, though, Dorothy Day believed that God called everyone to spiritual greatness through embodying our faith in daily life. "We are all called to be saints," Day affirmed. "We might as well get over our bourgeois fear of the name. We might also get used to recognizing the fact there is some of the saint in all of us. Inasmuch as we are growing, putting off the old man and putting on Christ, there is some of the saint, the holy, right here."[3]

Francis would have agreed with Dorothy Day's vision of activist sainthood. Realizing that he might be a model for others, getting in the way of their own spiritual growth, Francis always turned people to Christ, challenging them to follow Jesus's path of service, sacrifice, and hospitality. Like John the Baptist, his vocation was to live the message of Jesus and point others to the pathway of discipleship, whether as monks or householders.

Another activist mystic, Simone Weil, boldly challenges us to claim our own saintly and mystical activism: "Today it is not merely enough to be a saint, but we must have the saintliness demanded by the present moment, a new saintliness without precedent...a new revelation of the universe and of human destiny."[4]

God calls us to mystical activism, a deep-rooted spirituality inspired by our encounters with God and commitment to our spiritual practices, to bring beauty and healing to the world. Walking in the footsteps of Francis and Clare, we are called to be mystics of the here and now, not some distant age. When we look in the mirror, we may exclaim in disbelief, "Me, a saint? Are you kidding?" Within the concrete limitations of life, our gifts are lived out and expand as we devote ourselves to prayerful activism. Still we ask, recognizing our fallibility and limitations: Who am *I*

to be a saint, a mystic? Who am I with my temptations and falli-
bilities, impatience and intolerance, to be in God's presence and
claim my role as God's companion in healing the earth? What can
I do? The challenges are so great, and I am so small!

Saints and mystics often feel unprepared for their calling. Isaiah
shrank as he encountered the Living God, whose glory fills all
creation, "Woe is me! I am lost, for I am a man of unclean lips,
and I live among a people of unclean lips; yet my eyes have seen
the King, the LORD of hosts!" Cleansed by an angelic touch, but
still filled with a sense of inadequacy, Isaiah hears the voice of
God, saying, "Whom shall I send, and who will go for us?" With
full cognizance of his imperfections and limitations, Isaiah claims
his vocation as God's prophet, a mystical activist sent to heal his
nation, "Here am I; send me!" (Isaiah 6:5, 8).

Isaiah wasn't the only one who questioned his calling. Jeremiah
protested his youth and inexperience. Paul struggled with his
past. Peter wrestled with God's call to welcome strangers and
foreigners. Francis constantly struggled with the temptations of
the flesh and later his desire to mold and maintain the Order he
founded in his image. Saint and mystics are not perfect. Their
primary qualification is that they have, in fear and trembling and
doubt and wonder, said yes to encountering the Loving and Living
God and to following God's path in the concreteness of their lives.

Francis told his followers to walk on the good earth, forsaking
the privilege and comfort of horseback riding. He didn't want his
followers to be separated and superior to ordinary working class
people. To be saint is to plunge into the intricate, chaotic, and
wondrous interdependence of life, knowing our utter dependence
on God and the bounty of creation for every breath and for the
energy to share in God's vision of creative transformation. Saints

rejoice in their common humanity, knowing that God's word becomes flesh in fallible and ambivalent persons like ourselves.

We need saints and mystics for our time, and we need to claim our unique mysticism and sainthood, as we confront the apparently insurmountable crises of the twenty-first century: global climate change and species destruction, massive starvation and poverty, political unrest and dishonesty, pluralism and the betrayal of the faith by religious leaders, the growing gap between the wealthy and poor, the identification of materialistic success with self-worth, and the threat of pandemics challenging the rugged individualism of persons and nations. We need to recognize that we can be the change we want to see in the world through joining mystical moments with acts of activism and kindness.

As I pilgrimed through Assisi that morning, the town began to waken. Street cleaners and sanitation workers began their day. Innkeepers opened their doors and parents sent their children off to school. As the silent morning morphed into a busy day in which other pilgrims and tourists would soon fill the streets, I remembered the greeting that characterized Francis's encounters, "May God give you peace" as I quietly blessed each recently awakened passerby. And so, as we embark with Francis on our daily pilgrimages in mystical activism, I pray, "May God give you peace" on the path you travel, and may your adventures be plentiful as you bring peace and healing to this good earth.

IN THE SPIRIT OF SAINT FRANCIS

Each chapter will conclude with spiritual practices that will enable you to embody the spirit of St. Francis in your own life. Our calling is to be saints for our own time, inspired by the life of Francis and other spiritual teachers. We can't go back in history, nor do I suspect that we would want to return to Francis's time. We can awaken to the spiritual wisdom of those who have gone before us, allowing their experiences to inspire our unique spiritual vocations for our time. I have tried each one of these spiritual practices over the years. Some are ancient, others novel; I hope they will be guideposts for your own journey in the spirit of St. Francis.

It Will Be Solved in the Walking

If you are able, I invite you to go on a Franciscan walk, your own pilgrimage wherever you happen to live. Virtually every morning, I walk, sometimes with a prayer in my heart, other times simply embracing the beauty around me or ruminating prayerfully on a personal question or writing project.

In this simple practice, go for a walk with a sense of prayerful intentionality. After clearing your head with a few deep energizing and centering breaths, ask God to guide your steps and your reflections, giving you what you need to find direction in your current situation. Let questions and ideas emerge as you walk. Listen for divine guidance. Even those of us who have a clear sense of vocation have room to grow. I often pray, "Show me what I need to be doing today" or, "Guide my steps so that I might serve you more fully today" as I take my morning walk. You may receive a word of guidance and wisdom, a sense of openness to what the day will bring. Intentionally place the path you travel in the hands of a Wisdom greater than your own.

Pray the Peace Prayer

Though not written by him, this prayer attributed to St. Francis reflects the spirit of the thirteenth-century saint.

Lord, make me an instrument of Your peace;
Where there is hatred, let me sow love;
Where there is injury, pardon;
Where there is doubt, faith;
Where there is despair, hope;
Where there is darkness, light;
And where there is sadness, joy.
O Divine Master,
Grant that I may not so much seek
To be consoled as to console;
To be understood, as to understand;
To be loved, as to love;
For it is in giving that we receive,
It is in pardoning that we are pardoned,
And it is in dying that we are born to Eternal Life.

Take a few minutes each morning to breathe deeply, opening to God's Spirit energizing, enlivening, and inspiring. Experience God's Spirit giving life to your cells as well as your soul. After a few moments, read the prayer slowly and meditatively. Let the prayer soak in, permeating your spirit and guiding your steps throughout the day. You may choose to carry the prayer with you or post it where you can see it during the day. When you find yourself straying from your sense of God's vision for your life, return gently to the prayer without judgment, opening again to its guidance for your spiritual path.

Sharing the Peace of God

Francis encouraged his companions to greet everyone with "May God give you peace." Let that blessing fill your day. Whether spoken or silent, bless everyone you meet. Pray that every encounter brings peace and healing to the world. Experience your kinship with all creation, blessing the human and nonhuman world, including those you are tempted to curse. A life of blessing joins us with all creation and enables us to claim our vocation as God's beloved companions one moment at a time.

CHAPTER TWO

From Privilege to Prayer

> Do not store up for yourselves treasures on earth, where
> moth and rust consume and where thieves break in and
> steal; but store up for yourselves treasures in heaven,
> where neither moth nor rust consumes and where thieves
> do not break in and steal. For where your treasure is, there
> your heart will be also.... But strive first for the kingdom
> of God and his righteousness, and all these things will be
> given to you as well.
>
> (Matthew 6:19-21, 33)

My parents were shaped by their experiences of the Depression and World War II and, like many of their generation, they conveyed the impact of these national and global upheavals in their parenting. They knew what it meant to scrimp and save and sacrifice for the common good. In looking back at the Depression years, both of my parents could affirm "we weren't poor, we just didn't have any money!" as they remembered what it meant to live simply and share what you had with neighbors in need. While my father was serving in World War II as a lieutenant in the Pacific theater, my mother lived with rationing of gasoline, meat, and luxury items to support the war effort. They knew what it meant to defer gratification for the common good because they realized that, despite our differences in race, economics, and gender, we were all in this together. The war effort and our nation's future required all of us to sacrifice for the common good.

As a child, I was a charter member of the "clean plate club." We were told that if food was on our plate, we had to eat it, without exception. Our church actively supported mission efforts to Asia and Africa and every week I added a nickel, ten percent of my allowance, to "Pete the Pig," a little red plastic pig, dedicated to the work of American Leprosy Missions. When I was tempted to forgo certain items on my plate, I was told to "remember the starving children in China!" While my parents' generation's approach to parenting had its obvious limits, there was one clear message that was conveyed to us. Beyond the shibboleth of "waste not, want not," we learned that what we did with our resources, including our daily meals, had an impact on other people. My New Deal Democrat mother and small-town Republican father believed in the principles of stewardship that extended from household to community. We learned that generosity was essential to a good life, rights were balanced by responsibilities, and that the common good outweighed self-interest.

Having experienced poverty, my parents and many of their generation recognized their kinship with people less fortunate themselves. We were told we were getting "too big for our britches" when we boasted of our achievements or compared ourselves with those who struggled economically or intellectually. Deep down, my parents' generation knew, despite all their social and racial blind spots, that in any community, poverty and misfortune in one group affects the well-being of the whole. "There but for the grace of God go I" was invoked by my parents and many of their peers when viewing another's ethical, economic, or relational misfortune. They recognized that no person was immune from the slings and arrows of fate! That realization inspired them to acts of sacrificial living for the greater good of their communities.

No doubt, because of our ethnicity and rising middle-class status, we were privileged people, but we didn't let it separate us from vulnerable persons in the community. I recall my father, a small-town Baptist pastor, inviting migrant workers and homeless people to sleep in our garage, much to the consternation of his congregants. An Eisenhower Republican, he believed that this was mandated not only by human generosity and fair play, but by the gospel message of treating the least of these as Jesus.

Young Francis of Assisi was born into privilege. His father Pietro was a member of the rising merchant class, trading in cloth and fine fabric. His mother Pica was, by all accounts, intelligent, compassionate, and lovely. Francis's parents anticipated a great life ahead for their son and his brother Angelo. He would, no doubt, inherit and expand the family business and, along with his brother, support his parents in their old age. Though he was from what was then described as the commoners and not the nobility, Francesco's parents anticipated that their son would marry well, enjoy a comfortable life, be respected in the community, and ensure that his children would also be achievers.

Francis enjoyed the benefits of his economic and social status. Like many educated, upper-middle-class youths today, he experienced parties, good food, leisure to enjoy his friends' company, and the ability to imagine himself rising beyond his current status through acts of courage and loyalty on behalf of the regional elite. He never went a day without a good meal and a warm and comfortable place to sleep. He was known to be generous to friends and strangers alike, always saving a few coins to toss to beggars on the street. But there was a clear dividing line between his prosperity and their poverty. By the combination of chance, grace, and his father's ambition and hard work, his wealth and freedom of choice created a gulf between him and the impoverished people of Assisi, the surrounding countryside, and similar towns. No doubt, despite his personal generosity, Francis of Assisi, like many in our society, took his privilege for granted as God-given. Only later did Francis let go of his social and economic privilege so he could live in solidarity with all creation—rich and poor, human and nonhuman.

The Problems of Privilege

I am a person of privilege. My middle-class parents placed a high priority on education and, along with my aunt and uncle, subsidized my college and graduate school tuition. I lack for nothing economically. I have a good job, savings accounts and retirement plans, own a home, travel, and have the leisure to read widely and write daily. My overall health is good for someone in his late sixties and I can go wherever I want with few limitations. I work hard, but my schedule is flexible, enabling me to provide childcare, sports, and educational opportunities for my elementary school grandchildren. I also enjoy the privilege of being white in a society in which persons of color must deal daily with the realities of injustice, fear of harassment by law enforcement officers, and the impact of four centuries of slavery, Jim Crow laws, real estate redlining, and other "separate but equal" policies.

I am grateful for the privilege that enables me to study, write, and travel. The advantages of my birth and economic standing enable me to explore possibilities and actualize my God-given talents in ways denied to others as a result of the accidents of birth and political and economic upheaval. I also realize that my life is different from the majority world, where long hours at low wages, substandard housing, political uncertainty, child labor, and lack of nourishing and healthy food is the norm.

I have come to recognize that privilege can insulate as well as isolate. Despite our relative wealth and comfort, the realities of privilege can spiritually harm both the privileged and the marginalized, whose poverty is often the shadow side of our abundance. We who are privileged can gain the world and lose our souls. Our sense of entitlement and alienation from those who struggle contracts our spirits and renders us oblivious to the voice of God speaking through our human and nonhuman neighbors. We fail to realize that many of our greatest achievements are the result of advantages we neither deserved or earned just as many persons' poverty and failure come are the result of factors beyond their control. Initiative and hard work matter, but achievement is shaped by what we've been given, not just what we've earned. Tragically, the poverty of others is often connected to our own economic wellbeing.

The complacency of the privileged is at the heart of the prophet Amos's challenge to the wealthy of Israel. Amos observes that as much as we enjoy the benefits of economic privilege, our advantages can be factors in oppressing others as well as in destroying our own souls. The emotional and empathetic chasm separating the wealthy and their impoverished siblings will eventually lead to spiritual malnutrition among the wealthy.

Hear this, you that trample on the needy,
and bring to ruin the poor of the land,
saying, "When will the new moon be over
so that we may sell grain;
and the sabbath,
so that we may offer wheat for sale?
We will make the ephah small and the shekel great,
and practice deceit with false balances,
buying the poor for silver
and the needy for a pair of sandals,
and selling the sweepings of the wheat."...
The time is surely coming, says the Lord GOD,
when I will send a famine on the land;
not a famine of bread, or a thirst for water,
but of hearing the words of the LORD.
They shall wander from sea to sea,
and from north to east;
they shall run to and fro, seeking the word of the LORD,
but they shall not find it.
(Amos 8:4-6, 11-12)

Our failure to hear the cries of God's beloved children prevents us from hearing God's voice in worship and prayer. Our unwarranted judgment on the poor and vulnerable as somehow undeserving due to our perception of their lack of initiative and laziness leads to God's judgment on us.

Whenever we promote emotional and empathetic alienation from our companions, we endanger our own spiritual lives. Even our perceived goodness and piety can be spiritually hazardous if our spiritual equanimity and apparent ethical integrity tempt us to separate ourselves from those we perceive as less upright than ourselves. Jesus once told a parable that illuminates the dangers of self-righteousness, including our own.

> Two men went up to the temple to pray, one a Pharisee and the other a tax collector. The Pharisee, standing by himself, was praying thus, "God, I thank you that I am not like other people: thieves, rogues, adulterers, or even like this tax collector. I fast twice a week; I give a tenth of all my income." But the tax collector, standing far off, would not even look up to heaven, but was beating his breast and saying, "God, be merciful to me, a sinner!" I tell you, this man went down to his home justified rather than the other; for all who exalt themselves will be humbled, but all who humble themselves will be exalted. (Luke 18:12-14)

Righteousness and mysticism can also become a spiritual trap. Cognizant of his imperfections, and despite his spiritual celebrity status, Francis recognized that saints and sinners alike are subject to temptation. In fact, our affirmation of our saintliness can be the greatest obstacle to experiencing the full humanity of those around us. To see others as morally or spiritually inferior is place them in a subservient role, and create a type of spiritual exceptionalism, in which our sense of spiritual maturity is juxtaposed to their spiritual superficiality. No doubt, the recognition that saints and sinners alike stand in the need of God's grace is at the heart of the apostle Paul's "love chapter," "If I speak in the tongues of mortals and angels, but have not love, I am a noisy gong or a clanging cymbal" (1 Corinthians 13:1). As I reflect on Francis's life, I am sure that his physical asceticism and downward economic mobility, not to mention his regular practices of self-examination, were intended to affirm his solidarity with all God's beloved children, blessed and beautiful, finite and fallible. He knew his temptations and, in that knowledge, he never claimed superiority to those who were less "spiritually evolved" than himself.

It is obvious that privilege can separate us from others economically as well as spiritually and emotionally. Too often, we believe that we deserve our wealth and that we have earned our wealth on our own without the support and resources of others. From our perspective, the poor differ from us in terms of work ethic and skill, and are thus not our concern. We falsely perceive the poor as coming from another world and we often judge them to be responsible for their poverty. That surely is the point of Jesus's parable of the rich man and Lazarus see (Luke 16:19-31). The rich man can rightly claim he did nothing wrong. No doubt he supported the Temple and provided funds for a variety of benevolent organizations. If he laid off employees to add to his profit margin, he could state without guilt, "It's just business, nothing personal!" He simply didn't notice the beggar at his doorstep or the connection between his wealth and his neighbor's poverty. Yet, as Jesus notes, the chasm between them had moral and eternal consequences. Experiencing the torment of Hades, the rich man begs for Abraham's help, and receives a chilling response, reminding him that his lack of empathy not only distanced him from his poorer neighbors but from experiencing God's presence in his life.

Child, remember that during your lifetime you received your good things, and Lazarus in like manner evil things;

but now he is comforted here, and you are in agony. Besides all this, between you and us a great chasm has been fixed, so that those who might want to pass from here to you cannot do so, and no one can cross from there to us.

(Luke 16:25-26)

Francis knew that privilege can isolate us from our mortality and our sense of solidarity with the suffering of others. His divestment of his inheritance and refusal to travel by horseback joined him with the salt of the earth, often trampled by those with political, economic, and religious power. In contrast to persons with privilege, the poor and marginalized are daily reminded of the realities of death due to poor diet, inadequate health care, and, tragically, governmental action or inaction. Death is an everyday reality in Syrian refugee camps, inner city ghetto communities, and among Central American asylum seekers. The constant threat of death can lead to violence in marginalized communities; it can also lead to compassion and empathy that the privileged lack. In contrast, those of us who have pain relief, medical care, and good nourishment at our fingertips often forget that we, too, are dust and to dust we will return.

The Buddhist tradition tells the story of young Gautama's introduction to the realities of sickness and mortality. Like many parents, his father sought to prevent him from experiencing the harshness of life. Having received the prophecy that his son would become a great spiritual leader, Gautama's father sought to insulate him from realities that would inspire him to give up his family's legacy of wealth and power. But, on successive days,

Gautama ventured forth from the palace and was stunned by his encounter with an elderly man, a sick man, and finally a corpse. Overwhelmed by human misery, this sheltered young man discovered his spiritual calling when he encountered a monk on the fourth outing. Gautama left everything behind to follow the spiritual path of enlightenment.

Francis, like Jesus, knew that privilege without self-awareness can be spiritually perilous. Jesus's parable of the rich fool describes the foolishness of a farmer who neglected his neighbors and thought his wealth could produce true security and insulate him from the vicissitudes of life.

> The land of a rich man produced abundantly. And he thought to himself, "What should I do, for I have no place to store my crops?" Then he said, "I will do this: I will pull down my barns and build larger ones, and there I will store all my grain and my goods. And I will say to my soul, Soul, you have ample goods laid up for many years; relax, eat, drink, be merry." But God said to him, "You fool! This very night your life is being demanded of you. And the things you have prepared, whose will they be?" So it is with those who store up treasures for themselves but are not rich toward God.
> (Luke 12:16-21)

Death is the great equalizer that renders wealth and privilege powerless and irrelevant.

Death can plunge us into despair. Confrontation with our mortality can also, as Francis reminds us, awaken us to the beauty and wonder of God's creation and presence in our lives. Recognizing our mortality inspires us to experience our solidarity with suffering humanity. We are, as a plaque once erected on a Paris hospital noted, "the dying taking care of the dying." Francis would have recognized that within the tragedy of the COVID-19 virus is the challenge to all people and nations to realize our interdependence and recognize the illusion of ethnic, national, or economic separation. As Jesus asserted, the sun shines and the rain falls on the righteous and unrighteous—and the wealthy and poor—alike (see Matthew 5:45). Francis recognized the dangers of privilege and out of his own experience of conversion from privilege to prayer counseled his companions to go beyond class and status, emphasizing humility as the pathway of human heartedness and empathy.

From Privilege to Prayer

At the heart of Francis's spirituality is the quest to be Christ-like. The way of Jesus is the model for Francis's mystical activism. More than that, he experienced Jesus of Nazareth, the universal and intimate Christ, as our companion on the way. Christ's earthly life reveals what it means to go from power and privilege to solidarity and compassion. Paul's hymn to Christ from Philippians presents a vision of God, who could have chosen apathy but embodied empathy. In contrast to Aristotle's image of God as apathetic and unchanging, which has influenced many Christian theologians, God is the most moved, rather than unmoved, mover. God suffers with as well as for the world. Salvation is found in God's solidarity with us and our solidarity with one another. Listen to Paul's words of gratitude and counsel:

Let the same mind be in you that was in Christ Jesus,
who, though he was in the form of God,
did not regard equality with God

as something to be exploited,
but emptied himself,
taking the form of a slave,
being born in human likeness.
And being found in human form,
he humbled himself
and became obedient to the point of death—
even death on a cross.
(Philippians 2:5-8)

Our lifestyles and approaches to authority often reflect our images of God. For Francis, the power of God is made perfect in love, in intimate identification with human joy and sorrow. God is, philosopher Alfred North Whitehead affirms, the fellow sufferer who understands. Unlike our obeisance to kings, queens, and princes, we bow down to Christ out of love rather than fear. God's glory is birthed in a stable among oppressed and powerless community, not among those who rule by fiat and force.

Therefore God also highly exalted him
and gave him the name
that is above every name,
so that at the name of Jesus
every knee should bend,
in heaven and on earth and under the earth,
and every tongue should confess
that Jesus Christ is Lord,
to the glory of God the Father.
(Philippians 2:9-11)

Two moments from Francis's life reflect his own movement from privilege to prayer. According to his biographers, Francis found persons with the skin disfigurement we identify with leprosy loath-some and frightening. One day, as he encountered a person with leprosy, Francis was initially repulsed. Convicted by his emotional reaction, Francis dismounted and embraced the leper. Shortly thereafter, according to his medieval biographers, he traveled to a leper colony, where he begged forgiveness of them for his former alienation from them and left them with the kiss of peace. From then on, care for persons with leprosy became a unique focus on his ministry. In his own words, this movement from alienation to solidarity was pivotal in his spiritual transformation:

> The Lord led me to begin penance in this way: when I was in sin it seemed very bitter for me to see lepers. And Lord led me among them and I did mercy to them...and after that I did not wait long before I left the world.[5]

In embracing the leper community, Francis discovered that there is no "other." Beneath the distressing disguises of others, whether homeless persons, immigrants, or bullying political leaders, we will discover the face of Christ. Living in the constant presence of Christ, we experience our solidarity with all creation, especially its most vulnerable human and nonhuman members.

Francis wished to be one with the poor of the earth. In a practice I described earlier, we observe a second moment, reflective of Francis's movement from privilege to prayer in his counsel that his spiritual companions travel by foot rather than on horseback. In Francis's time, difference in status between the military and civilian life was reflected in the contrast between knights on horseback and common foot soldiers. In contrast, the knight of Christ sought to be one with the poor and vulnerable. Embracing simplicity reflected solidarity with all humanity. Francis would not "lord" it over anyone! Followers of Christ's way go beyond the superficial differences, the externals that get in the way of our relationships with our fellow humans, to oneness in the body of Christ, where our joys and sorrows are one.

Prayer as an Act of Solidarity

Throughout my life, I have focused on prayer as a symbol of solidarity, because prayer is grounded in the profound interdependence of life. Our prayers of gratitude remind us that no one is self-sufficient. Our gifts and talents emerge from our relationships —the persons and institutions that have supported us, as well as the earth's bountiful providence—that inspire and undergird any achievement on our part. From this perspective, the self-made person is the most pitiable precisely because they, in their lonely individualism, think they can go it alone without any help from God or their fellow creatures. This sense of self-sufficiency collapses when we face a health crisis, death of a life companion, a professional setback, a pandemic, or the realities of aging and mortality.

Prayer links us with all creation. Our gratitude inspires relationship and connection. Recognizing that we are truly one in spirit and flesh with all creation, we are inspired to move from self-interest to global concern. We discover that in an interdependent universe, others have been the answers to our prayers, coming along at the right time to provide comfort and counsel, and that we can be the answer to others' prayers, sharing the gifts we have received so that others might flourish in body, mind, spirit, and relationships.

Francis came to view his whole life as a prayer. As we will discover in our reflections on Francis's "Canticle of Creatures," prayer joins us as healing partners with all creation. In a world where everything fits together seamlessly, every thought, word, and act can bring healing and beauty to the world. All creation praises its Creator. All things find their origin and completion in God's love. The meek are blessed precisely because they recognize their dependence on the generosity of God and creation, and out of their dependence, the humble commit themselves to be Christ to others, claiming their vocation as God's companions in healing the earth. The privileged become blessed in prayerfully letting go of their sense of superiority and seeing themselves as united with humanity and all creation, sharing their possessions and working for a world in which everyone has a fair chance to enjoy the fruits of this good earth.

In the Spirit of St. Francis

Francis teaches us to live in a world in which there is no "other," no creature, human or nonhuman, alien to us. We are bound together in an intricate web of relatedness, in which our well-being is interconnected. The world, even beyond the church, is the body of Christ, in which we celebrate each other's joy and mourn each other's suffering. Let us embrace the wondrous interdependence of life, in which difference leads to appreciation and diversity to beauty.

Beyond Appearances Is Unity in Christ

From the outside, differences abound and our perception of

differences often leads to division. Yet, deep down, beneath life's experiences is our common identity as God's beloved children. The true light enlightens each person and all creation. We are all joined in God's loving light. In this exercise, let your prayers lead you from alienation to unity, especially with those whom you might find repulsive and disgusting. We may discover angels in our own "lepers."

Begin this exercise in a time of silence, breathing deeply the oxygen you share with your earthly companions. With each breath, experience yourself as part of one Great Breath, the Spirit of God, flowing in and through you and all things. Once you feel centered and connected with God and all creation, visualize those with whom you are most closely joined: spouses and partners, children and grandchildren, friends and companions, coworkers and members of your congregation, and others who are near and dear to you. With each breath, experience your unity with them. Now, look more deeply beyond appearances to experience their holiness as God's beloved children. Experience God's light shining forth from them, regardless of its hiddenness. Pray for their well-being and wholeness.

Next, visualize a few persons from whom you are alienated. These may be persons of a different social standing, economic class, race or ethnicity, or political perspective, or even your own family. These may be public figures whom you identify with the forces of chaos and destruction. These are your lepers! I must admit that I feel disgust when I see certain political figures appear on the news. My experience of their holiness is eclipsed by their behavior and my negative judgments. As you visualize these persons, open to the reality beneath the surface and hidden by your disgust. Can you see the light of God emerging from its disguise? Can you experience their deeper holiness, hidden as it may be from you and perhaps from them? Experience your sense of connection, despite your apparent alienation, as you pray for their wellbeing and wholeness.

Francis experienced his deep unity with members of a leper colony. He discovered that there is no "other" and that he was connected to persons with leprosy by the intricate connectedness of God's love. We are filled with gratitude for the gifts each of us brings. We celebrate each other's unique beauty and pray that each of us discovers God's love and shares the love that creates a world in which all are pilgrims and none are strangers.

The Great Thanksgiving

Prayers of gratitude join us with all creation. They may even inspire us to see God's presence in life's challenges and recognize that although God is not the source of evil and suffering, the tragic beauty of life exists as part of God's creative wisdom and love, embodied in every moment of life. I have long treasured the prayer of Dag Hammarskjöld, former General Secretary of the United Nations:

> For all that has been—thanks!
> For all that shall be—yes![6]

God's bounty gives birth to every moment of experience and, as Francis "Canticle of the Creatures" affirms, divine wisdom is present in fire, water, air, and earth, and in all living beings. Without God's loving creativity moving through all things, not one thing would exist nor could we achieve anything. Even death is part of God's good creation and we can face our mortality with gratitude and praise.

In this spiritual practice, simply say "thank you." Let that be your prayer throughout the day and in every encounter. Let it be part of inner dialogue as well as well as your sharing with others. Count your blessings throughout the day and let your blessedness join you with others and inspire you to bless the world. During the pandemic, I led a service of Morning Prayer on Zoom. All of us were homebound as a result of self-sequestering due to the coronavirus. We shared gratitude, hopes, and blessings despite being homebound. We discovered that physical distancing did not mean spiritual or social distancing. We were still united in God's creative love.

Out of gratitude comes the great yes to life in its wondrous diversity. Gratitude inspires us to bring beauty to our relationships, local and global. Our yes to life joins us with others. Let us, like Mary of Nazareth when she was confronted by the angel Gabriel, say yes to God's invitation to do greater things than we imagine and pass our gifts on to others with every breath and action. Our yes inspires us to move from gratitude to justice and compassion. Our privilege becomes the catalyst to shared experiences with the vulnerable and the willingness to let go of our wealth for the well-being of those around us.

CHAPTER THREE

Reforming Spirituality

> I appeal to you therefore, brothers and sisters, by the
> mercies of God, to present your bodies as a living sacri-
> fice, holy and acceptable to God, which is your spiri-
> tual worship. Do not be conformed to this world, but be
> transformed by the renewing of your minds, so that you
> may discern what is the will of God—what is good and
> acceptable and perfect.
>
> (Romans 12:1-2)

Less than a mile down the hill from Assisi is the church of
San Damiano. According to Francis's biographers, the future
saint retreated regularly to the chapel to pray for guidance for the
next steps of his spiritual journey. The church was seldom used
because of its dilapidated condition. As Francis prayed one day,
he heard a message from God. He experienced the crucified Jesus
addressing him personally, providing him direction for his next
steps, "Rebuild my church, which is in ruins." Being sensate in
orientation, and deeply rooted in the concreteness of the physical world, Francis initially took his mystical experience literally,
assuming the divine message was directed to refurbishing the
church of San Damiano. Francis set himself to the task of being a
church mason and carpenter, purchasing supplies with the money
available to him, and rejoicing in the opportunity to serve Jesus
in a tangible way.

Francis was so dedicated to church rebuilding that he refurbished two other nearby chapels, San Pietro and St. Mary of the Angels, before it dawned him that God had something greater in mind for him. Francis came to believe that God called him to rebuild the troubled and chaotic church spiritually as well as physically.

The church of his time had drifted far from the Galilean vision of hospitality, sacrifice, and peacemaking. Francis's expanded vision of spiritual renewal based on the life of Jesus transformed his sense of mission and inspired him, first, to gather a small cadre of friends as spiritual companions, and then initiate religious orders for women and men whose mission humbly challenged the church he loved and its religious leadership to align their practices with those of Jesus.

I appreciate Francis's initial focus on rebuilding the local church. In an interdependent universe, you can't separate the physical and the spiritual, and the immediate and global. Famed Massachusetts politician Tip O'Neill once said that all politics is local. The same is true of spirituality. Although we must never place boundaries on the circumference of God's love, we must also recognize with St. Bonaventure, one of Francis's followers, that the center of divine love is everywhere and most particularly right where we are. Salvation is global, but the hundredth sheep must be returned home for the ninety-nine safely in the fold to find wholeness.

For the past few years, as a local pastor on Cape Cod, Massachusetts, I have been spiritual advisor and, at times, cheerleader, for our congregation's capital campaign. Our two-hundred-year-old sanctuary and various other parts of our congregation's home need refurbishing, upgrading, and renovation to sustain our mission for the decades ahead. Throughout the process, I have reminded our congregation's leadership that "brick and mortar are holy, too" and that our building improvements are primarily about expanding our mission and welcoming the local community for generations to come as well as providing spiritual nurture for our current membership. We are a local church, with specific responsibilities for the spiritual nurture of our community, but we also seek to live by a global perspective, affirming that our parish is the whole earth. Like Francis, we recognize that what we initially think is concrete and local is ultimately spiritual and radiates across the community, nation, and planet. We need to refurbish our church building while also transforming our mission to respond to the spiritual crises of our time.

For Francis mysticism leads to mission. Hearing God's voice propelled him to action: first to restore San Damiano and then to begin a spiritual revolution in the church. He discovered in the process a holistic spirituality that embraced brick and mortar, body, mind, spirit, relationships, and the social order.

Rebuilding and Reforming

Although Francis's first biographer, Thomas of Celano, described the mystic activist as "always new, always fresh, always beginning again," Francis did not set out to be an ecclesiastical or social reformer.[7] In the footsteps of reformers and prophets, past and present, he experienced the living God. With that encounter, like Isaiah, Jeremiah, Martin Luther, Martin Luther King, Jr., and Dorothy Day, Francis received God's vision of a new kind of spirituality, grounded in the affirmation of an alternative reality to the injustice, inhospitality, and materialism of his time. Seeking to live in accordance with the Gospel lifestyle of Jesus and his first followers, Francis discovered the profound dissonance between the powerful and wealthy religious empire of the Roman church, the legacy of Constantine's marriage of church and state, and the simple and egalitarian ministry of Jesus of Nazareth. The Western church of Francis's time possessed immense wealth, wielded extraordinary political and military power, ruled by force, and promoted persecution and war against heretics and infidels.

During Francis's time, Jesus's vision of peace on earth, goodwill to all, whose strength lay in the vulnerable power of love had been eclipsed by the love of power, the desire for theological uniformity, and the need for institutional survival and expansion. The pilgrim Gospel of Jesus and the early Christian movement had given way to the doctrinal and ecclesiastical traditionalism and the "desire to acquire" land, wealth, and power. The Roman church was at war, promoting Crusades against Islam, a costly military undertaking that required appropriating the financial and human resources of local municipalities and common people. This is a temptation of the church in every age, to put power over love, orthodoxy over compassion, and authority over spiritual transformation.

Despite its many good works and deep spiritual heritage, in its quest to preserve and expand its ecclesiastical and political influence, the church succumbed to the three temptations, described in Jesus's sojourn in the wilderness following his baptism, the desire for material prosperity, the need for absolute security, and quest for unilateral power to secure the common good.

Francis's Alternative Vision

Inspired by his calling to an evangelical lifestyle, Francis presented an alternative vision of faith to the hierarchical power of popes and princes. The tattered and powerless monastic reflected a contrasting understanding of discipleship and fidelity to that of the wealthy institution that initially nurtured his faith. Although he was an obedient son of the church, seeking to be a knight of Christ and aiming to restore the gospel way of life among God's people, Francis was simultaneously a threat and an image of hope to the leadership of the church he loved.

Francis did not seek to undermine the social and religious order of church and government. His revolutionary spirituality embraced people of every class and social station: rich and poor, powerful and powerless alike. I am sure that Francis was aware that his itinerant ministry depended on the generosity of merchants, farmers, tradespeople, who were committed to the system he challenged. Therefore, despite his countercultural orientation, he recognized that sustaining his mission was dependent on, and to a certain extent complicit in, the economic and spiritual order he sought to transform. I believe Francis's understanding that he benefitted from the economic initiative of others led him beyond polarization to a sense of community with those whose lifestyles he challenged. Francis's affirmation of the solidarity of life along with awareness of his own imperfections and temptations enabled him to embrace those he critiqued as God's beloved children, whose spiritual wellbeing was of upmost importance to him despite their differences.

Francis's mission called people beyond greed and materialism to the deeper realities of hospitality, kindness, and faith. Francis also sought to redefine divine and human power. God ruled the world by love and not unilateral power. To follow the way of Jesus, God's beloved son, was to see every relationship in terms of

God's love for creation and embody loving power at home, in the church, and in politics. The One who sacrificed everything to live among us was his guidepost for power relationships, whether in the monastery or the larger church.

Francis discovered the perfection of love embodied by Jesus's journey to cross. Jesus suffers the agony of crucifixion and shares in the pain of the world. The true God, the God of Jesus, is experienced in common cause with the least of these as well as in challenge to the greatest. With mystics throughout the ages, Francis experienced what Rabbi Abraham Joshua Heschel described as the divine pathos, God's identification with suffering humanity, especially those whose pain was caused by the injustice and inhumanity of the powerful. Francis sought to challenge anything that stood in the way of people experiencing the joy of God's presence in their lives, even if this meant challenging the values of the church he loved. Like reformers and prophets throughout the ages, Francis knew that institutions, even churches, have a vested interest in the status quo.

Francis knew that holding on to wealth, power, and institutional survival makes conservatives of us all, obscuring the pilgrim origins of our faith and separating us from the most vulnerable members of our community. Discovering his unity with all God's children, Francis recognized that although his way of life and message might afflict the comfortable as well as comfort the afflicted, there are times that the comfortable also need grace and understanding to claim their own spiritual healing. Conversely, the marginalized and dispossessed need to claim the power of missional living that awakens them to their worth as God's beloved children, created in the divine image.

Francis's reformation involved the renunciation of security and familiarity. While spiritual reformation eventually leads to a world where all are pilgrims and none are strangers, the path to spiritual and cultural reformation begins with Francis's recognition that he and his followers must also be pilgrims and strangers, not conformed to the values of the world in which they live and open to constant creative transformation at the hand of God. In living by another set of values than the world around them, Francis and his followers became a light on a hill, shedding light on ecclesiastical and economic corruption and providing a path to healing and transformation for persons and institutions.

The Reformation Must Continue

If Western Christianity had embraced Franciscan simplicity, solidarity, and spirituality, the schisms of the sixteenth century might not have occurred. A church that is "always new, ever fresh, and always beginning again," welcomes diverse and innovative visions and judges their merit from the perspective of God's vision not human self-interest and defensiveness. Much of the spiritual unrest that inspired the Protestant Reformers involved practices that Francis challenged three centuries earlier: the centralization of wealth and power among the ruling class, the church as an economic institution, clergy affluence joined with professional laxity, authoritarian and hierarchical approaches to leadership, the identification of church and state, the church as an instrument of persecution and violence toward outsiders, and defining God in terms of power rather than love. While Martin Luther lacked the peaceful spirit of Francis, both spiritual reformers sought to recall the church to the grace-filled wellsprings of vital faith, the evangelical zeal of the open-spirited first century followers of Jesus.

Recognizing the temptation to absolutize institutional power to the detriment of living faith, the most perceptive of the sixteenth-century Luther's followers proclaimed *ecclesia semper reformanda est*, "the church is always reforming." That motto applied equally to the Reformed and the Roman churches. Three centuries before Luther, Francis visualized a constantly reforming faith, on the move, initiating spiritual novelty to respond to the novelties of the environment.

As spiritual children of Francis, his spiritual companion Clare, and reformers throughout the centuries, we need to rebuild, restore, and reform the church of our time in all its diversity, possibility, and fragility. We need to commit ourselves to lives of constant conversion, guided by God's vision of the peaceable and just realm. Just as few persons experiencing the profound changes of their time could grasp the impact of the victory of Constantine and his joining of church and state, the fall of the Roman Empire, the Crusades, and the printing press on Christian institutions, twenty-first century followers of Jesus are wrestling with the impact of the internet, social media, postmodern pluralism, cultural incivility and polarization, globalism, and rapid technological change on our beloved institutions. We are also struggling to understand and respond to the collapse of Christendom and the rise of religious pluralism in the twentieth and twenty-first centuries.

Finding a Center in the Storm

The only spiritual, technological, and cultural constant in our time is the rapidity of change and our inability to fathom the impact of what Alvin Toffler described in the 1960s as "future shock," the impact of rapid change on our personal, institutional, and cultural psyches. Looking at one aspect of my own life, I purchased my first cell phone 1999. At the time, cell phones had only one purpose, telephone communication. Twenty years later, I take photographs, look up information, play games, chart road trips, send text messages, make notes for lectures and books, and write on my cell phone. My cell phone answers questions and serves as my alarm clock. I even use it to call people!

I grew up listening to one television channel, received news from Edward R. Morrow and Walter Cronkite, and breaking news only occurred in times of national catastrophe. Today, cable and digital media gives me hundreds of options for real-time information on forest fires, political protests, mass shootings, and air crashes. "Breaking news" occurs every fifteen minutes, leaving us in a constant state of anxiety and suspense, wondering what the next "crisis" will be.

In the religious world, instead of the Neapolitan options—Protestant, Catholic, Jewish—of the 1950s, I can access religious rituals from hundreds of wisdom traditions at a tap of my phone or laptop. Past is no longer prologue in terms of personal spirituality as many persons leave the religions of their families of origin, become adherents of other faiths, practice hybrid spiritualities using practices from a variety of spiritual traditions, or abandon religious traditions altogether without feelings of guilt or remorse. The fastest growing religious preference in North America is the "nones," persons who identify with no specific religious tradition. The intellectual and moral credibility of Christianity among young people has dramatically fallen due to coverups of clergy sexual misconduct, persecution of the LGBTQ community, denial of climate change and the theory of evolution, and the self-identification of the majority of conservative Christian leaders with political leaders who appear to disparage the traditional Christian—or human—virtues of fidelity, honesty, civility, and compassion.

Once at the center of family life and personal morality, now Christianity is now culturally at the margins, irrelevant for the most part to peoples' daily lives. Moreover, the communication systems and social media intended to bring us together have been factors in incivility, polarization, and the retreat of persons and political parties into their own personal silos, denying any outside and dissonant information that might challenge their agreed upon facts.

Although the simple thirteenth-century saint gives no specific blueprint for our time, I believe that our faith traditions need the wisdom of Francis, appropriate to our unique social, political, and spiritual context. In conversation with the humble prophet of Assisi, we may discover a mystical activism that transforms the current marginal religious status we lament into frontiers of spiritual and global adventure. We may also become aware of and respond to the deepest needs of the majority world, struggling for self-determination and survival, and our own cultural, racial, and economic privilege. Like the pilgrim from Assisi, our calling is to become mystic activists, whose commitment to spiritual practices and encounters with God inspire us to claim our vocation as God's companions in healing the world, embodying a gospel of inclusion of humankind in its wondrous diversity.

Where All are Pilgrims and None are Strangers

Francis did not claim that his way of life could be universalized in a monolithic fashion. Francis always pointed beyond himself to the Living Christ present on the cross and throughout creation. Francis was a child of his time and his spiritual path was forged in the unique economic, ecclesiastical, and technological realities of the twelfth and thirteenth centuries. We are children of our own unique economic, technological, and ecclesiastical time, and must embrace and convey the wisdom of Francis and other mystical activists in accordance with God's presence in our lives and world.

Quoting Bishop Mark Dyer, spiritual guide Phyllis Tickle notes that "every five hundred years the church feels compelled to hold a giant rummage sale" and that today "we are living in and through one of those five-hundred-year sales."[8] Tickle believes that the church needs to discard the "cumber" that prevents it from navigation toward God's future.

As a couple who are pondering downsizing to a smaller home in the next few years, my wife and I realize the importance of decluttering and refurbishing to increase the resale value of our home and to make it possible to live joyfully in our next home. Contemplating my four thousand books and well-furnished home, I am beginning to ask myself "Which of these possessions are truly essential to my life? What must I give up to embark gracefully on the journey ahead?" I love my books and many have strong sentimental and intellectual value, charting my academic and pastoral journey. But I know that moving forward means letting go of much of my beloved library even though it is painful. This is ultimately a spiritual issue, calling me to reflection and transformation long before the movers arrive. It is about discovering what is truly important and finding a spiritual center that transcends ownership, economics, and familiarity.

Moving forward spiritually, individually and institutionally, also means letting go of what we once felt was necessary but now bars the way to deeper understandings of God's vision for our future. Reflecting on his process of letting go of beloved traditions to embrace the Living Christ, the apostle Paul notes:

> When I was a child, I spoke like a child, I thought like a child, I reasoned like a child; when I became an adult, I put an end to childish ways. For now we see in a mirror, dimly, but then we will see face to face.
> (1 Corinthians 13:11-12)

Francis's reformation required renunciation, an intentional letting go of what encumbered him materially and spiritually so that he could follow the way of Jesus and live in a world where there is no "other." When I look at what Francis's counsel to Christians and Christian institutions might mean today, I believe his reformation challenges us to focus on experiencing God's ever fresh and ever current wisdom and not holding onto past certainties. It means traveling light theologically and spiritually, embracing the wisdom of diversity, and recognizing that although change means death to values and beliefs that no longer serve the church's mission, transformation also is the gateway to resurrection and abundant life. It means listening to the cries of the poor, the petitions of youth, such as Greta Thunberg and the Parkland students as they demand environmental action and safe schools. It also means doing something surprisingly countercultural for today's Christians, making prayerful contemplation the basis for activist transformation. Our prayer forms must be grounded in listening to God's voice at the margins and among the voiceless as well as in our own restless sighs too deep for words.

Letting Go and Traveling Light

Francis let go of economic security and personal privilege to follow the way of Jesus. He also learned to travel light without possessions to embrace the life-giving simplicity that joined him with the common people and enabled him to be spiritually open to every encounter. His spiritual experiences could have inspired him to seek a settled life as a spiritual guide or administrator of a monastery or a place of importance at the pope's side. Instead, Francis chose an itinerant spirituality in which he let go of theological and institutional baggage to be faithful to God's moment by moment vision. Francis did not directly challenge the theology and doctrine of the church nor critique those who were called to more stable religious and domestic vocations. The Franciscan way of approaching the world simply relativized theological doctrine and ecclesiastical order, bringing them down to earth in real life situations that put persons ahead of theological correctness and healing ahead of liturgical uniformity.

As a pioneer in interfaith hospitality, Francis did not demonize the "Saracen," the Muslim community, but reached out to the political leader of a faith with which his religious institution was at war. Francis paid little attention to heresy hunting and put personal well-being ahead of abstract doctrine. Though embedded in the Trinitarian faith of the church, Francis was guided by God's living wisdom and word not entrenched doctrine and tradition.

Francis treasured tradition and embraced novelty, knowing that the Living God is also on the move. His cross-shaped spirituality reminded him that God is found in suffering and solidarity with humankind and not apathetic individual ecstasy. The Christ of Calvary inspires us to let go of any theological or ecclesiastical encumbrance that stands between us and our neighbor. Perhaps the saint of Assisi, despite his apparent theological orthodoxy, maintained doctrinal flexibility because he realized, as do other spiritual reformers, that doctrine is dead without love and that historically doctrines have been employed to judge, alienate, excommunicate, and persecute. The way of the cross joins us with all creation, in its vulnerability and suffering, most especially with those who are discarded and marginalized, whether religiously, economically, or in terms of identity. We are one with whomever our culture deems as "lepers," regardless of doctrinal dictum. To be faithful to Jesus, the church must become, as liberation theologians assert, a church of the poor and common rather than merely the wealthy and powerful.

Traveling light today inspires us to put persons ahead of programs and policies and relationships ahead of doctrinal certainty. While seeking the treasure of divine wisdom found in theological reflection, liturgical practice, and spiritual emphases, we recognize that our treasures are in earthen vessels. Filled with humble spirits, the pilgrim church is both in the world and in contrast to the world's ways. We honor new insights in the areas of science, literature, human development and sexuality, and recognize the wisdom of other spiritual traditions along with the critiques of spiritual outsiders and refugees from lifeless orthodoxy and toxic religion. Nothing is foreign in a world in which God speaks through Brother Sun and Sister Moon, a menacing wolf, and a scorned leper.

Openness to the world awakens us to constant reformation, believing that divine inspiration is found beyond as well as within our religious institutions. Living faith is growing faith. Even Jesus grew in wisdom and stature, and so must we and our institutions as we trust that God will guide us through the twenty-first-century spiritual wilderness, showing us what we need to change, jettison, and affirm and reminding us that through all life's changes, nothing can separate us from the love of God in Christ Jesus our Savior (see Romans 8:38-39).

Embracing Theological and Spiritual Diversity

Many of us may be generous relationally, but theologically and spiritually greedy. We believe that there is only one way to worship, pray, meditate, or understand God. We judge other paths as simply wrong or inferior to our own. In the Baptist tradition of my youth, we judged those who were not fully immersed as lacking the fullness of baptism. In their failure to follow what we believed to be New Testament practices, they might, we thought, even be missing out on salvation. Other Christians speak of their neighbors missing the fullness of the gospel because they lack direct apostolic succession or understand their sacraments symbolically rather than tangibly as the body and blood of Christ. In the church of my youth, we assumed that non-Christians were unsaved and destined for hell if they did not accept Jesus as their personal savior. We had doubts about the Roman Catholics' salvation and I am sure the Roman Catholics had their doubts about ours!

Francis was a committed follower of Jesus. It is also clear that he embodied a "generous orthodoxy," to use a phrase popularized by theologians Brian McLaren, Hans Frei, and Fleming Rutledge. He held fast to the embodied and crucified Christ but was open-hearted in terms of his response to diverse expressions of faith. This is not unusual for mystics and activists who honor tradition while judging authentic spirituality in terms of our experiences and responses to the Holy.

Although he was obedient to papal policies, Francis was opposed to the spiritual and physical violence associated with the Crusades. As a person of peace, he objected to religious coercion and violence associated with the Crusades and heresy hunting and advised his own followers to practice hospitality and civility when responding to persons of other faiths.

In 1219, Francis was present at one of the pope's Crusades in northern Egypt. During a time of truce between the Christians and Muslims, Francis sought to visit the sultan with hopes to convert Sultan Malik al-Kamil to the way of Jesus. Although Francis failed in his quest, he and the sultan became friends, listening to one another's witnesses and respecting each other's spirituality. In a time of mutual suspicion, hatred, and violence, Francis and the sultan broke down religious barriers and experienced the holiness of one another as they engaged in interfaith dialogue.

Francis's visionary spirituality challenges us to embody generous and welcoming theological reflection. On the one hand, God is the reality in whom we live and move and have our being. The true light of God enlightens everyone. Every person, culture, and ethnic community is touched by divine wisdom and can be a source of revelation for us. An open-spirited faith is willing to embrace the spiritual riches of diverse Christian and non-Christian visions, congruent with our own understandings of God. On the other hand, God's reality transcends every faith tradition. In our fourteen billion year old, trillion galaxy universe, no tradition, including our own, can fathom the height and breadth of divine wisdom. Our theological treasures are in earthen vessels, finite and imperfect. We can treasure our sacraments, theological visions, and spiritual practices, but need to remember, to use Buddhist imagery, not to confuse the moon with the finger pointing toward the moon.

The reformed church is always reforming. The church is always a pilgrim church, open to constant transformation at the hand of God. Faithfulness to the way of Jesus calls us beyond our theological, ethical, ecclesiastical, economic, and spiritual homelands to meet Jesus on the road to greater and greater understandings of God and the world.

Cross and Resurrection

There are times when reformation and renunciation feel like death. Change doesn't come easy because change means letting go of familiar beliefs and behaviors to embrace God's future vision. Following the reforms of Vatican II, many traditional Roman Catholics complained, "Who stole my church?" as changes were made in religious practices, feast days, religious requirements, and worship styles. Some free church Protestants experienced liturgical confusion as their congregations began following the lectionary, seasons of year, and liturgical colors. "We're becoming just like the Catholics!" they moaned. The changing role of women in the church and professional life leading to changes in marital roles have felt like a mini-death to adherents of binary gender roles. Marriage equality and hospitality to the LGBT community, and the rise of ethnic and religious diversity, has led to grief at the loss of the good old days and the rise of white supremacist groups. Whether it involves losses in religious, cultural, liturgical, or social privilege, change elicits grief and longing for the way things were. The way of the cross, the giving up of power and privilege to be attentive to God's vision, is painful. But the way of the cross is the way of life as it opens us to new ways of experiencing God's presence in the world. For Francis and his spiritual companion Clare, the cross was God's invitation to share in the suffering of the vulnerable. Just as Jesus experienced the pain of the cross, we move from apathy to empathy, seeing Christ in the poor and vulnerable, and recognizing that despite our apparent differences, we are one in Christ. The cross breaks down every theological, economic, and ethnic barrier we place between ourselves and others.

Reformation leads to resurrection. No longer conformed to the world of injustice, privilege, and alienation, we experience God's creative transformation that joins us with all creation. There is a restlessness in reformation that reflects the divine restlessness of the Hebraic prophetic tradition. Francis experienced this holy restlessness as he traveled the highways and byways of Italy and as he confronted religious leaders. He knew that divine perfection is found in compassion and responsiveness to the pain and joy of the world. Francis knew that the God who guided his steps providentially brought opportunities for reconciliation and healing into his life on a daily basis. Francis discovered that God is no recluse, unconcerned with time and history. The Living God is the source of novelty and adventure. The God of the prophets and mystics joins eternity with constant change in God's quest to heal the world.

WALKING WITH FRANCIS OF ASSISI

WALKING WITH FRANCIS OF ASSISI

The moral and spiritual arcs of history call us forward, reminding us that God's vision of Shalom is a polestar and not a resting spot. Yes, we need moments of quiet contemplation, Sabbath times, and restorative self-care. These moments of retreat give us perspective and patience with the long haul of history. In silence, we are joined with all creation, including our apparent "opponents." Our contemplations also find fulfillment in lively partnership with God in healing the world.

The story is told of Yale Divinity School professor Halford Luccock. As he walked across the Yale green, a youthful evangelist confronted him with the question, "Are you saved?" After pausing a moment, the professor responded, "Every day." Francis and Luccock both recognized that the spiritual journey is a continuous process of sanctification, of growth and adventure, and not a final, static destination. In describing the Franciscan way, Clare of Assisi, a spiritual leader in her own right, asserted that spiritual growth involved "allowing your entire being to be transformed into the image of the Godhead itself."[9]

Humility is at the heart of spiritual reformation, whether it is personal, congregational, or political. Humility reminds us of our imperfection and finitude and prevents us from claiming privileged moral or spiritual status. We share a common humanity, and dare we say, divine identity, with those who hang onto tradition, fear change, and claim power over others. We recognize that we too have our comfort zones and are tempted to claim superiority over our neighbors. We too are tempted to our own versions of law and order and our perquisites of racial and religious privilege over our commitments to love and community. In this dissonance between where we are and where God calls us, we experience

God's restlessness moving through us energizing and inspiring us, with Francis, to embody God's realm "on earth as it is in heaven."

IN THE SPIRIT OF ST. FRANCIS

Francis challenges every generation to reform and rebuild the church, using the materials of tradition and innovation at its disposal. God is still speaking to us through the cross and resurrection. Where we see no way ahead for ourselves or the church, God provides a way forward

Visualizing Rebuilding the Church

In this spiritual practice, I invite you to join St. Francis at the church, of San Damiano or a holy place to which you are drawn. For this exercise, you may choose to meditate on some of the images of San Damiano found on the internet or in Assisi guidebooks. After a time of quiet centering breathing deeply the presence God and then blowing it gratefully out into the world, visualize yourself in the church of San Damiano. Place yourself before the cross of Jesus, contemplating God's presence in your life and the suffering of the world. Experience Jesus as your companion as you ask for God's wisdom. Visualize your local congregation, if you have a church home, as well as the church in North America or the nation where you live.

In your imagination, visualize where the church of our time, either your home church or the church as a totality, is in ruins, physically, spiritually, or culturally. Experience God calling to you with the words "rebuild my church." See yourself rebuilding the church in community with Christians of all times and places in the wondrous diversity of the Christian family.

Let images emerge reflecting ways in which your own religious home can be rebuilt and reformed. Which images most deeply touch your spirit as you ask God for your personal calling as a rebuilder and reformer? As you continue to ask for divine guidance, visualize ways you can use your gifts, talents, and resources to be God's companion in renewing the church. Visualize Jesus as your companion, providing the inspiration and resources you need to be faithful to your calling. Give thanks for the opportunity to serve God as a companion in renewing your community and the church universal.

The Way of the Cross as the Call to Adventure

In this exercise, once again locate yourself at San Damiano or some other sacred spot. Imagine Christ calling you to experience his empathy with the pain of the world. Where is Jesus the Christ experiencing pain in our world? What images come to mind when you reflect on those experiencing pain and vulnerability? As I practiced this exercise, my imagination turned to persons experiencing homelessness on Cape Cod, over thirty of whom died in the past year; the victims of school shootings at Sandy Hook and Parkland; children separated from their parents by the government; persons fleeing the genocide perpetrated by the government of Myanmar; families separated from dying relatives in the time of pandemic; and children and young people diagnosed with cancer, as my own son was in his late twenties. Ironically, I felt the loneliness, anxiety, insecurity, and fear of a political leader whose character and policies I view as misguided and dangerous! Let yourself feel their pain and hopelessness as well as their hope or the hope of loved ones for healing and transformation. Train your senses for signs of resurrection and new life as you ask Jesus to be your companion in showing you where you can be his partner in responding to the pain of the world, bringing new life and defeating the forces of chaos and death. Claim your role as a resurrection companion of Jesus.

CHAPTER FOUR

A World of Praise

Praise the LORD from the earth,
    you sea monsters and all deeps,
fire and hail, snow and frost,
    stormy wind fulfilling his command!
Mountains and all hills,
    fruit trees and all cedars!
Wild animals and all cattle,
    creeping things and flying birds!
...

Let everything that breathes praise the LORD!
Praise the LORD!

(Psalm 148:7-10, 150:6)

Pivotal moments in our spiritual journey can come at any time. Our lives, as Francis discovered, involve a process of continuous conversion. They also involve widening the circle of ethical and spiritual consideration. God constantly speaks to us in the events of our lives, whether through a voice piercing the silence of a chapel, a synchronous encounter with a person suffering from leprosy, or the flight of a sparrow above our heads. Each moment can be an epiphany, awakening us to new understandings of ourselves and God's vision for us and the world. We can even hear God's voice in the dog sleeping at our bedside, the cat lounging on our lap, scenes of polar bears swimming for their lives in the Arctic, or in Native American holy spaces desecrated by the construction of oil pipelines. Perhaps we can even hear the voice of God whispering amid the maelstrom of pandemic. Francis discovered God in worms and wolves; he challenges us to see God among the least of these in the nonhuman world and then respond with acts aimed at healing the planet.

Growing up in the congregation's manse, I was a pious Baptist child. I took the stories of Jesus seriously. I believed Jesus could feed five thousand from fives loaves and two fish. I believed in the power of prayer and prayed about everything from the health of a neighbor to God's guidance in finding a lost baseball in the backyard. Trailing clouds of glory, as Wordsworth says, my world was enchanted with messages coming from the morning songs of robins, August thunderstorms, and the words of Scripture. On a few occasions I experienced a mystic sense of Jesus as my companion as I walked the streets of our small town in California's Salinas Valley. I talked to our family's chickens and developed a personal relationship with the king of the barnyard, a Rhode Island Red rooster I named "Pitter" (his spouse was "Patter").

As a young child, I discovered that my mystic vision of the world was exceptional among the Baptist elders of our community. One weekend, my parents left my brother and I with a pious Baptist lady, Bertha Orr. Mrs. Orr owned a lively poodle named Taffy with whom I struck up an immediate loving relationship. We played together all weekend—fetch, racing on the beach, and cuddling on the rug. At one point in the weekend, I asked Mrs. Orr, "Will Taffy go to heaven?" It seemed a reasonable question for God-intoxicated child, raised on images of heaven and hell, to ask. Mrs. Orr's response astounded me and ironically set me on a path that eventually led to a new understanding of God. "You better talk to your father about this. Of course dogs don't go to heaven. Jesus didn't die for their sins. Your dad will set you straight." I was humiliated, but worse than that, I began to doubt the goodness of God, or at least the way we understood God in our church. Didn't God love Taffy? Didn't God love what was important to me? How could Jesus, who loved the birds of the air and the lilies of the field, not love a lively poodle? If Taffy wasn't in heaven, was heaven truly a place of joy and celebration?

Seven hundred and fifty years earlier, St. Francis asked similar questions: If Jesus cared for the nonhuman world of worms, flowers, and birds, shouldn't we? And, if God loves the world, shouldn't we seek to live in harmony with all of God's creatures, adapting our behaviors to embrace them as companions on our spiritual journeys?

Francis's first followers recorded the story of a dangerous wolf who tormented the citizens of the Umbrian village of Gubbio. The villagers were afraid to go out into the countryside without weaponry. They sent hunters out to kill the wolf, but still the wolf eluded them and continued to terrorize the village, frightening children and attacking sheep. To the astonishment and fear of the villagers, Francis went into the woods to confront the wolf. When the wolf saw Francis, the wary wolf initially charged at him, but was stopped in his tracks when the saint made the sign of the cross and then admonished the wolf for his violent behavior. He commanded the wolf to choose the path of peace, forbidding it from attacking the townspeople and their domestic animals. The holy man then returned to the village, inviting the villagers to welcome the wolf into their midst, ensure that he was fed and treat him with respect. Deep called unto deep and the wolf experienced a spiritual conversion in his encounter with Francis. A greater conversion occurred when the villagers welcomed the wolf as a fellow creature, creating a bond between the wolf and the community, in which each supported, protected, and cared for the other.

More Than a Birdbath!

Pope John Paul II proclaimed St. Francis the patron saint of those who promote ecology in 1979. In 2015, Pope Francis began his encyclical *Laudato Si: On Care for Our Common Home* with the words of St. Francis:

> *Laudato Si', mi' Signore*—"*Praise be to you, my Lord.*" In the words of this beautiful canticle, Saint Francis of Assisi reminds us that our common home is like a sister with whom we share our life and a beautiful mother who opens her arms to embrace us. "Praise be to you, my Lord, through our Sister, Mother Earth, who sustains and governs us, and who produces various fruit with coloured flowers and herbs."[10]

For eight centuries, Francis's "Canticle of the Creatures" has inspired mystics, spiritual leaders, schoolchildren, and social activists alike. In the spirit of Psalm 148, the Psalmist's hymn to creation, which we will explore later in this chapter, Francis invites us to live in a world of praise in which all creation declares the glory of God and every creature is to be reverenced as a reflection of Divine Wisdom:

Be praised, my Lord, through all your creatures,
especially through my lord Brother Sun,
who brings the day; and you give light through him.
And he is beautiful and radiant in all his splendor!
Of you, Most High, he bears the likeness.
Praise be You, my Lord, through Sister Moon
and the stars, in heaven you formed them
clear and precious and beautiful.
Praised be You, my Lord, through Brother Wind,
and through the air, cloudy and serene,
and every kind of weather through which
You give sustenance to Your creatures.
Praised be You, my Lord, through Sister Water,
which is very useful and humble and precious and chaste.
Praised be You, my Lord, through Brother Fire,
through whom you light the night and he is beautiful
and playful and robust and strong.
Praised be You, my Lord, through Sister Mother Earth,
who sustains us and governs us and who produces
varied fruits with colored flowers and herbs....
Praised be You, my Lord,
through our Sister Bodily Death,
from whom no living man can escape....
Praise and bless my Lord,
and give Him thanks
and serve Him with great humility.[11]

Francis affirmed that we live in a world of praise, a sanctuary of
the Spirit, in which each creature's experience declares the wisdom

and creativity of God. For eight centuries, people of all ages have been captivated by stories of Francis's nature mysticism and his reverent interaction with the nonhuman world. Doves and crows delighted in the saint's presence, listening with greater attention than many of Francis's human companions! According to his biographer Thomas of Celano, Francis regularly blessed creatures of all kinds with the sign of the cross as well as with spoken benedictions. Once, after preaching a sermon to the birds, Francis "accused himself of negligence because he had not preached to them before." In years to come, Francis "carefully exhorted all birds, all animals, all reptiles, and also insensible creatures, to praise and love the Creator, because daily, *invoking the name* of the Savior, he observed their obedience in his own experience."[12]

On another occasion, while preparing to give a homily, Francis noticed that swallows were chirping with such great joy that his human audience could not hear his words. Francis admonished his feathered companions, "My sister sparrows, *now it is the time* for me to speak, since you have already said enough. *Listen to the word of the Lord* and stay quiet and calm *until the word of the Lord is completed.*" And verily the sparrows listened with reverence and attention rivaling that of his human audience.[13] Taking seriously the scriptural words "I am a worm and not a man," Francis discerned the holiness of the worms he encountered in the course his pilgrimages. Thomas of Celano notes that "that is why he used to pick them up from the road and put them in a safe place so that they would not be crushed by the footsteps of passersby."[14] In speaking of Francis's relationships with the nonhuman world, Thomas continues:

Fields and vineyards,
Rocks and woods,
all the beauties of the field,
flowing springs and gardens,
earth and fire, air and wind;
all these he urged to love of God and to willing service.
Finally, he used to call all creatures
by the name of "brother" and "sister"
and in a wonderful way, unknown to others,
he could discern the secrets of the heart of creatures
like someone who had already passed
into the freedom of the glory of the children of God.[15]

Francis lived in an enchanted and God-filled universe in which heaven and nature truly sing God's praises and inspire us to praise as well. Long before Walt Disney's filmmaking, the Saint of Assisi believed that humans and nonhumans could communicate with one another and that nonhuman animals possessed inner emotional lives. In contrast to the disenchanted universe of the modern world in which the nonhuman world exists primarily to serve human interests, Francis believed that earth, sea, sky, air, and every living thing possessed inherent value apart from human interests. Implicit in Francis's world view is what today's theologians, philosophers, and now scientists call "pan-experientialism" or "panpsychism," the affirmation that the universe is alive and experience is universal.

Freed from the shackles of the modern materialistic and dualistic worldview, scientists are discovering that experience of one form or another is universal. In the spirit of indigenous and aboriginal peoples, Celtic spiritual guides, and today's earth-centered spiritualities, scientists have found that flowers and trees interact with their environments, sensing threat as well as benefit. Bees have been found to be innovative rather than repetitive in their responses to their companions in the hive. Crows have been observed learning new tasks, overcoming obstacles, and managing deferred gratification. Crows can wait for as long as five minutes in front of desirable objects—longer than my grandchildren!—to earn a reward. My goldendoodle, Tucker, can identify our moods, recognize nearly one hundred words, and gallop joyfully across Cape Cod dunes, feeling God's pleasure with every step. Descartes's and Newton's mechanistic worldview has given way to a living universe, which calls forth empathy in ourselves and our nonhuman companions. While there are many levels of experience ranging from the comparative simplicity of the atomic and cellular to complexity of the mathematical and mystical, truly the rocks truly sing out and heavens declare God's glory.

Francis embodied an empathetic spirituality. His mystical experiences gave birth to experiences of enchantment, empathy, and reverence in relation to the nonhuman world. He experienced the holiness of worms, sparrows, and wolves and they could in turn feel his love for them. Enchanted by Francis's empathetic spirit, the wolf of Gubbio felt himself loved. He knew intuitively that Francis was different. He was no longer afraid nor did he wish Francis harm. The sign of the cross created a spiritual bond that transformed the wolf from predator to a companion. Nature alive, praising its Creator, inspired Francis and his followers throughout the ages to see the holiness of all creation and respond with reverence and respect.

The Ethics of Praise

Although my editors and I are always thorough in our proof-reading, sometimes an editorial mistake, overlooked by the author and his literary team, can be the source of wisdom. A reader of one of my books recently sent me a note, observing an error in my transcribing of Isaiah 40:6. Instead of Isaiah's "all flesh is grass," I had written "all flesh is grace." For Francis, my error would have been revelatory of a deep spiritual truth. Creation is grace. The transitory world of flesh and blood, whether feathered or scaled, mammal or marsupial, mediates God's grace and reveals God's wisdom and providence by virtue of its very existence. Deep down everything praises God and can be a source of personal and community transformation. In the spirit of Jesus, Francis knew that sparrows and wildflowers can teach us what it means to depend fully on God's grace.

Praise inspires empathy. The opposite of praise is apathy and inability to experience wonder at each atom of God's creation. Praise is inspired not only by God's grandeur but by the beauty of creation. Praise is grounded in our experiences of joy and suffering. As the prophet Amos says, if you fail to hear the cries of the poor and vulnerable, you will be unable to experience God's wisdom and guidance (see Amos 8:4-12).

In the lively and enchanted world of Francis, ethical decision-making is grounded in our recognition of others' feelings of joy and celebration and pain and sorrow, including the joys and sorrows of the nonhuman world. Spiritual companions of Francis, twenty-first-century Buddhist monks have "ordained" trees to prevent them from being razed by developers. Recently, students at Union Theological Seminary in New York confessed

humanity's sins in relationship to plants and flowers.[16] One seminary student tweeted:

> Today in chapel, we confessed to plants. Together, we held
> our grief, joy, regret, hope, guilt and sorrow in prayer;
> offering them to the beings who sustain us but whose gift
> we too often fail to honor. What do you confess to the
> plants in your life?

Francis would have honored their recognition of God's presence
in the world of flora and fauna. No doubt Francis mourned the
pain inflicted on nonhuman animals and recognized that willfully
destroying God's world was a sin against its Creator.

One of my spiritual mentors, African American mystic-activist
Howard Thurman, relates a painful story from his youth in
Daytona Beach, Florida. It was an autumn day and young Howard
was raking leaves for a white store owner. As he raked leaves in
a pile, the store owner's four-year-old daughter decided that she
would play a game with Howard. Whenever she saw a brightly
colored leaf, she scattered the whole pile to show it to Howard.
She did this several times until Howard told her to stop. When
she kept scattering leaves, Howard said he would tell her father.
Upset by his threat, she jabbed him with a straight pin. When he
cried out in pain, the girl responded, "Oh Howard, that didn't
hurt you. You can't feel."[17]

You can't feel! That is the heart of the modern mechanistic
worldview that sees nature as an object to be exploited without
consideration of its inherent value or the suffering we perpetrate
on our nonhuman companions. Apathy is the source of violence,
exploitation, and incivility. This emotional apathy, the belief that

others can't feel or have no rights, relates to humans we consider enemies, outsiders, or different in race, ethnicity, gender, or religion from ourselves. In the spirit of Jewish mystic and theologian Martin Buber, others become "its" to manipulate and use rather than "thous" to respect and revere.

Francis knew better than today's apathetic materialists and insatiable consumers. Although the saint did not articulate a systematic ethics of reverence for life, Francis's lifestyle revealed his insight that humans and nonhumans alike can feel pain as well as joy. He knew the wolf of Gubbio was afraid as well as angry. Francis recognized that his threats were based on fear of injury. The worm underfoot does not want to be smashed by our careless meanderings. The swallows want to sing and rejoice, praising God with melodious hymns and joyful chirps. What we judge as instinctual in the nonhuman world may reveal a deeper experience of joy, contentment, and foresight.

Those who are forgotten, abused, disinherited, and unjustly treated can feel! This applies to nonhumans as well as humans! There is a solidarity in suffering that joins spirits and is heightened by our recognition that when the least of these sufferers, God is in pain. God is, as the philosopher Alfred North Whitehead asserts, "the fellow sufferer who understands."[18] God is also the joyful companion who celebrates with all creation. Francis saw God's presence in all things and all things embraced in God's experience. This is not "pantheism," which assumes the world and God are one reality, but what today's theologians describe as "panentheism," the recognition that the world is the body of Christ in which God's Spirit breathes through and creates in all things and embraces the experiences of all things. God is in all things and all things are in God.

The ethics of praise and empathy challenge us to become awakened, woke, and aware of the pain and joy of others. Francis would surely understand the truth in Linda's affirmation of her husband Willy Loman, Arthur Miller's tragic figure in *The Death of a Salesman:* "I don't say he's a great man. Willy Loman never made a lot of money. But he's a human being, and a terrible thing is happening to him. So attention must be paid."[19]

Attention leads to empathy, empathy leads to ethical reflection, and ethical reflection leads to activism to respond to suffering wherever we observe it. Francis paid attention and challenges persons and institutions to do likewise. Inattention leads to marginalization, manipulation, and misuse. In contrast, attention leads to ethical action. Consider what we often forget in our business and political decision-making—impoverished neighborhoods, the homeless and working poor, the welfare of children seen primarily as consumers, swamplands and their nonhuman residents, and microscopic plankton, the foundation of maritime survival. While Francis did not have a clearly defined political policy that can be identified with a current political party, he had something more profound based on his mystical vision of the graceful and dynamic interdependence of life. Mysticism inspires us to pay attention and then support the lives of our nonhuman as well as human companions. Mystical attention enlarges our hearts and minds, and motivates questions such as: Why is this child crying? Why is this animal screaming? Why are polar bears swimming for their lives and the right whale near extinction? Why is this parent desperate and anxious? Why are this community and its residents hopeless?

Paying attention to the reality of suffering challenges us personally and politically to embody acts of healing and wholeness.

While Francis recognizes that we are all complicit in the suffering of our fellow creatures through the very fact of ensuring the survival and wellbeing of ourselves and our loved ones, we need to minimize both human and nonhuman suffering. For privileged North Americans, this has profound political, lifestyle, and economic implications. We need to pay attention to our diets, not just in terms of our physical health but the environmental impact of processed and transported foods as well as our consumption of meat and poultry. Given his affirmation of the nonhuman world, we can speculate that Francis would be at forefront of combatting climate change by both his personal example and his counsel to ecclesiastical and political leaders. As we will see in upcoming chapters, simplicity and world loyalty are values we must cultivate as individuals, communities, and nations. Joined with all creation, our praises challenge us to go beyond materialism, individualism, and nationalism to claim our vocation of rebuilding the earth.

In the Spirit of St. Francis

We live in a world of praise. As the prophet Isaiah discovered, the whole earth is full of God's glory (see Isaiah 6:1-8). The glory of God, reflected in all creation, inspires wonder, gratitude, and amazement to those who open their senses to holiness. Our experience of God's glory also invites us to an ethic of reverence for life in its diverse manifestations. Spirituality inspires activism to heal the earth.

Gratitude for the Earth

Praise and gratitude go hand in hand. We praise God for the beauty of the earth and give thanks for God's blessings abundantly strewn throughout the world. Gratitude, in turn, leads to a life in which our sense of being blessed inspires us to claim our vocation interpersonally and politically as God's companions in healing the world. In this spiritual exercise, take fifteen minutes each day to contemplate the wisdom of Psalm 148 and 150:6. Begin with a time of silence, breathing deeply your connection with the world around you: Feel the breath of life that enters you as part of a great cosmic breath, the Spirit of God moving in all things. Experience the wonder of breathing and your very existence. Feel yourself rooted in creation, dependent on the world around you and contributing by your life to the world beyond you. Read meditatively the words of Psalm 148 and Psalm 150:6:

> Praise the LORD!
> Praise the LORD from the heavens;
>   praise him in the heights!
> Praise him, all his angels;
>   praise him, all his host!
> Praise him, sun and moon;
>   praise him, all you shining stars!
> Praise him, you highest heavens,
>   and you waters above the heavens!
> Let them praise the name of the LORD,
>   for he commanded and they were created.
> He established them forever and ever;
>   he fixed their bounds, which cannot be passed.
> Praise the LORD from the earth,
>   you sea monsters and all deeps,
> fire and hail, snow and frost,
>   stormy wind fulfilling his command!

Mountains and all hills,
    fruit trees and all cedars!
Wild animals and all cattle,
    creeping things and flying birds!
Kings of the earth and all peoples,
    princes and all rulers of the earth!
Young men and women alike,
    old and young together!
Let them praise the name of the LORD,
    for his name alone is exalted;
    his glory is above earth and heaven...

Let everything that breathes praise God.

As you read the passage, let images of an enchanted and praise-filled world fill your imagination. Let this passage shape the way you look at the world. Look beyond appearances to see the inner divinity of the world. Listen for the Deep Spirit of God speaking through a praise-filled world.

Out of your appreciation for the world, reflect upon how you can share in God's vision of Shalom, especially as it relates to global climate change and species extinction. How can you speak for the earth? Where do you need to act to honor the world of praise? How might your prayers and praise turn to grace-filled healing activity in your daily life?

Living with the "Canticle of the Creatures"
According to one of his biographers, Francis not only immersed himself in prayer. His whole life became a prayer. As part of creation, our prayers are joined with the "groaning" of creation

(see Romans 8:22). We are not alone and lost in the universe, our lives are upheld by the prayers of the universe. Even the stars pray, as theologian and spiritual guide Jay McDaniel proclaims. The groaning of creation, as the apostle Paul recognizes, is of one reality with our own personal yearning for healing and wholeness for ourselves and the planet.

In the spirit of your meditation on Psalm 148, prayerfully contemplate the wisdom of Francis's "Canticle of Creatures." After a time of silent gratitude, recite the prayer twice, letting it soak in. What images, phrases, or words come to mind. Perhaps one word, phrase, or word speaks to your spirit. Let that phrase, word, or image be your lens for experiencing the world.

> Be praised, my Lord, through all your creatures,
> especially through my lord Brother Sun,
> who brings the day; and you give light through him.
> And he is beautiful and radiant in all his splendor!
> Of you, Most High, he bears the likeness.
> Praise be You, my Lord, through Sister Moon
> and the stars, in heaven you formed them
> clear and precious and beautiful.
> Praised be You, my Lord, through Brother Wind,
> and through the air, cloudy and serene,
> and every kind of weather through which
> You give sustenance to Your creatures.
> Praised be You, my Lord, through Sister Water,
> which is very useful and humble and precious and chaste.
> Praised be You, my Lord, through Brother Fire,
> through whom you light the night and he is beautiful

and playful and robust and strong.
Praised be You, my Lord, through Sister Mother Earth,
who sustains us and governs us and who produces
varied fruits with colored flowers and herbs....
Praised be You, my Lord,
through our Sister Bodily Death,
from whom no living man can escape....
Praise and bless my Lord,
and give Him thanks
and serve Him with great humility.[20]

Explore the various aspects of creation Francis identifies in the "Canticle of Creatures": sun, moon, wind, air, water, fire, land. Experience the holiness of these elements. Ask for God's guidance in terms of how you can honor the holiness of our planet's elements. What first step, or new step, is God inviting you to take in responding at a community and public policy level to protect the basic elements of the earth? Such earth care is vital today, given the warming of the oceans, the destruction of coral reefs, the acidification of the seas, the pollution of air, destruction of the biosphere, and depletion and contamination of the soil. Our creation mysticism leads to creation affirmation, protection, and nurturing as we experience our solidarity with the groaning of our planet's air, earth, sea, and sky.

Global Confession

Every faith tradition has pathways of confession, ranging from the Jesus Prayer ("Lord, Jesus Christ, have mercy upon me a sinner") to communal prayers of confession and private confession with a spiritual guide or priest. While some people were scandalized by seminary students asking plants for forgiveness, our personal and communal healing requires transformed living, which emerges through repenting our sins against creation and accepting God's graceful forgiveness and invitation to kinship with creation.

In this time of confession, quietly reflect on the relationship of your actions to planetary destruction. What lifestyle decisions contribute to climate change and species destruction? Where have you neglected or caused the suffering of your nonhuman companions? Where do you need greater empathy with creation?

Ask God's forgiveness and ask God to give you awareness of your sins against creation. Symbolically ask a nonhuman creature to awaken you to the cries of creation and ask for forgiveness for you sins against the planet. In response, accept God's grace and commit yourself to a life of planetary healing.

CHAPTER FIVE

The Gifts of Downward Mobility

Blessed are the poor in spirit, for theirs is the kingdom of heaven.

(Matthew 5:3)

Blessed are you who are poor,
for yours is the kingdom of God.
Blessed are you who are hungry,
for you will be filled.

(Luke 6:20-21)

When I was eleven, my world fell apart. Up until then, I lived in the paradise of small-town Salinas Valley, California. Although my family was middle class, my father, as the local Baptist pastor, was respected in the community. We lived in the congregation's parsonage, a spacious and airy home just a few blocks from church, school, and Little League games. Life was predictable and secure until my father lost his job due to a congregational controversy. Within a month, we were forced to move a hundred miles north to metropolitan San Jose, where we had no social standing and were living off our parents' modest savings until my father secured a position as a security guard at a semiconductor plant. For a short period of time, we received food baskets to supplement our family's meager financial resources.

Where once everyone recognized me as an up-and-coming baseball player and Baptist pastor's kid, now no one knew my name. I didn't fit into the diverse neighborhood of hardscrabble kids. Internalizing the economic and social trauma, I came down with an undiagnosed illness which kept me in bed for two weeks.

I must confess that until I finally acquired a certain level of spiritual stature and financial security, my childhood experience shaped my response to finances. Despite my professional successes, I wondered, "Is this enough for a rainy day? What if I lose my job? Will my family be plunged into poverty?" For years, finances were a source of tension between my wife, raised in economic security and privilege, and myself.

I realize that I am not alone in my quest to achieve a healthy attitude toward finances.

Most Americans never seem to have enough money, despite comfortable lifestyles and pension plans. Perhaps because of our culture's spiritual malnutrition, we are fixated on consumption, ownership, and financial security, lured by the promise that "whoever dies with the most toys wins." Deep down, we know that money can't buy love or happiness, but we act as if it will fill the void, providing us with security and protection from the trials and tribulations of life. Sadly, many people connect financial prosperity with spiritual growth and poverty with lack of faith.

In moments of reflection, many of us realize that despite our financial concerns, we are truly privileged. Although we have enough resources for a comfortable lifestyle and the leisure and money to go on spiritual retreats, cultural events, and order books online, we regularly measure our worth in terms of our mortgages, spendable income, and the value of our homes, stock portfolios, and retirement plans, oblivious to the fact that the majority of the world lives from paycheck to paycheck and meal to meal without an economic, social, or communal safety net. Our privilege is in stark contrast to millions in poverty in the richest country on earth and the realities of global malnutrition and political instability, much of it due to the impact of climate change and economic manipulation by developed nations. We need a change of heart reflected in changed interpersonal behaviors and political decision-making. As we look at our personal and national economic life, the apostle Paul's counsel speaks directly to us: "Do not be conformed to this world, but be transformed by the renewing of your minds, so that you may discern what is the will of God— what is good and acceptable and perfect" (Romans 12:2).

Now over fifty years since the collapse of my idyllic childhood, I realize that those experiences of the early 1960s were a blessing as well as a curse. My anxiety about financial security has opened my heart to the cries of the poor. I realize that I can't isolate myself from those whose lives are vastly different from mine in terms of economics, access, and housing. We are all in this together. Though our privilege can lead to apathy and isolation, the realities of climate change and the growing gap between the rich and poor in the United States and around the world challenge me to look beyond my personal welfare to the wellbeing of my grandchildren but also that of children everywhere whose lives will be shaped by economic and environmental decisions we make today. The world of praise, described by Francis's "Canticle of the Creatures", reminds us that we are all connected in an intricate fabric of interdependence and that our choices ripple across the planet bringing joy and sorrow and life and death to persons we will never meet.

Gospel Simplicity

In a world of widespread poverty and powerlessness, prior to the emergence of what today we describe as the middle class, Francis and Clare were born into privilege. Despite the pressure to follow the mores of their social and economic class, Francis and Clare had the freedom to choose their way of life. Confronted by demands of the Gospel, these saints-to-be chose poverty and downward mobility.

Following the mystical call to rebuild the church, Francis refurbished both San Damiano and the Portiuncula. Following Mass one day at the rebuilt Portiuncula, Francis asked the parish priest to explain the gospel to him. As the priest explained the day's gospel line by line, once again Francis experienced life-changing divine guidance:

> When he heard that Christ's disciples should not possess gold or silver or money, or carry on their journey a wallet or a sack, nor bread nor staff, nor have shoes nor two tunics, but that they should preach the kingdom of God and penance, the holy man, Francis, immediately exalted in the spirit of God. "This is what I want," he said, "this is what I seek, this is what I desire with all my heart."[21]

Francis patterned his life and the Franciscan movement after the gospel simplicity and humility of Jesus, whose self-emptying and letting go of power and prestige was at the heart of his divinity. Divine power is found in downward mobility and identification with human suffering, not in weaponry, status, or comfort. God's love for the world is expressed in solidarity with the least and with those whom New Testament scholar John Dominic Crossan describes as a "kingdom of nuisances and nobodies." In contrast to the opulence and military power of the caesars and emperors throughout history and the religious leaders of his time, Francis sought to embody the deeper power of God's healing presence within the realities of poverty and powerlessness.

Exaltation emerges from sacrifice and solidarity. Jesus embodied a radically different lifestyle than that of the heads of church and state. In Francis's time, some church leaders dressed in the finest clothing, lived in comfortable homes, and managed vast fortunes despite the poverty of most worshippers. In contrast, Francis discovered that the glory of God is found is identification with the salt of the earth, the most vulnerable people, the poor, disabled, and leprous. The incarnation of Christ means that Christ is one of us, not lording it over like presidents and prelates, but living among the poor and dispossessed. A poor Christ reveals what Abraham Joshua Heschel describes as "the divine pathos," God's intimate experience of the world's pain and suffering. God feels our pain and rejoices in our celebration. Foolish by the world's standards, Francis, Clare, and their followers sought the way of holy poverty or spiritual simplicity that breaks down walls and builds bridges with all God's creatures. Better than none, equal to all in need of God's grace, and depending on God's gifts for life itself, Francis and Clare found God in the least of these. They served Christ by letting go of power in order to become siblings of all creation. Clare chants her own praise to Gospel simplicity in harmony with her older spiritual companion.

O blessed poverty,
who bestows eternal riches on those who love
and embrace her!

O holy poverty,
to those who possess and desire you
God promises the kingdom of heaven
and offers, indeed, eternal glory and blessed life!
O God-centered poverty,
whom the Lord Jesus Christ
Who ruled and now rules heaven and earth,
Who spoke and things were made,
condescended to embrace before all else![22]

In letting go of wealth and prestige, Francis and Clare found everything! In poverty, they experienced abundant life! No longer burdened by fear or worry, they could, like the like lilies of the field and birds of the air, praise God with heart and voice, and love their neighbors as themselves. With nothing to protect, they could share everything they had as God's abundant life flowed through them to bless the world.

The Privilege of Poverty and the Poverty of Privilege

A good friend of mine believes that Paul's counsel, "have the mind of Christ," is a Christian koan, a paradoxical statement used by a Zen master to thwart our rational machinations and shock us into spiritual transformation. Throughout the day, he asks himself, "What is the mind of Christ in this situation? How can I see this event with Jesus's vision?" Striving to understand the mind of Christ in terms of self-emptying (kenosis) and letting go of ego has inspired my friend to simplify his life, volunteer at the homeless shelter, and work in the community to promote legislation that provides opportunities for vulnerable persons to receive housing, job training, and health care.

Francis and Clare invite us to ask similar questions in relationship to our possessions, "How can I practice simplicity in my life? How can I let go of my possessions to be faithful to God? In what ways can I live simply so others can simply live?" Moreover, Francis and Clare ask us to experience our economic situation and the living situations of the majority world and the poor through the mind of Christ.

As we ponder the nature of gospel living in response to the holy simplicity of Francis and Clare, we might also take note of the curious counsel, "Be careful what you pray for." Francis and Clare challenge us with the question, "Do you really want to live more simply? Do you really want to make the changes necessary to live an ecologically sustainable life? Do you want to downsize in terms of assets and political power so others can be uplifted? What are you willing to give up for the survival of future human and nonhuman generations?"

As a householder with responsibilities toward my church, family, grandchildren, and community, I am, regardless of my commitment to holy simplicity and spiritual and domestic decluttering, caught up in the materialism and consumerism of our time. Locking the doors of my home in a safe Cape Cod neighborhood is not just a sign of prudent behavior but also can be a way of shutting myself off from perceived threats of persons from different economic strata whom I believe might do me harm. I realize that many of my behaviors are fear-based rather than love-based. In having something to protect, I build walls against those who might wrest it from me. Francis and Clare remind me if I am to live the gospel life, I must take to heart Jesus's blessings:

"Blessed are the poor in spirit" (Matthew 5:3).

"Blessed are the poor" (Luke 6:20).

To be faithful to God and the Franciscan vision, I must seek to be "poor in spirit." Poverty of spirit means letting go of status, attachment to possessions, and spiritual and intellectual privilege to embrace my solidarity with the vulnerable of the earth. For Francis and Clare, poverty of spirit meant recognizing our absolute dependence of God for life itself and every gift and achievement. The poor in spirit recognize the radical interdependence of life in which our lives emerge from the gifts of the environment and persons around us and, in turn, contribute to those around us.

The Gospel life challenges us to balance our personal security and comfort with our care for the earth and its peoples. Mahatma Gandhi said that there is enough for our need, but not for our greed. How do I provide a safe and nurturing home for my grandchildren's daily visits while attending to the needs of other peoples' grandchildren? How do I place my money at the availability of institutions that support the vulnerable and neglected while ensuring that my wife and I experience a secure environment? How do I live simply but also ensure that my children and grandchildren attend safe schools and live in safe neighborhoods? As I ponder these questions, the title of Thomas Merton's *Conjectures of a Guilty Bystander* describes my own inner conflict. I am not ready, and may never be ready, to follow in the footsteps of Francis and Clare, or Peter Maurin and Dorothy Day, who gave up the comforts of the middle class—economic security, privacy, and individualism—to live among the poor in

Catholic Worker houses. Still, there is much I can do as a guilty bystander, beginning with letting go of the sense of otherness and tearing down intellectual and emotional walls that separate me from those who differ economically, politically, ethnically, and intellectually. I must be willing to give up many of my creature comforts for others to enjoy the economic and educational privileges I take for granted.

The poverty of privilege occurs when it separates us from others, trapping us in the illusion of our safety and security, when in fact the world is on fire economically, epidemiologically, and ecologically. Privilege promotes apathy toward the needs of others and, in so doing, shrinks our spiritual lives, leading to a famine of hearing God's deepest messages to us. The illusion of privilege is the belief that we are immune from suffering, aging, death, and economic insecurity. Yet, many persons have discovered that the solidarity of suffering and insecurity may be the open door to spiritual transformation. In becoming poor in spirit, we experience God as the fellow sufferer who understands and the loving companion who rejoices.

Jesus proclaims, "blessed are the poor." Neither Jesus nor Francis and Clare idealized the enforced poverty of the masses. They recognized the despair, anguish, and hopelessness of the politically and economically powerless. They were aware that poverty can crush the spirit and rob children of their imaginations. They also realized, as liberation theologian and Franciscan Leonardo Boff claimed, that "to be radically poor [is] to be fully human."[23] The poor in spirit and the economically impoverished know they can't make it alone. They depend on the powers outside themselves for their survival and wellbeing and recognize their solidarity with fellow sufferers. Fully dependent on others and ultimately on God, we go beyond individualism to become members of God's beloved community and desire that all God's children—and the nonhuman world—be honored and nurtured, that the hungry be fed and the poor hear good news and the wealthy be liberated from the chains of possession and power.

The Gifts of Simplicity

Acquisition and possession define twenty-first-century consumerist culture. Community has given way to rugged individualism. Generosity has been supplanted by greed. Empathy has been eclipsed by apathy. This is obvious in the growing gap of rich and poor, the incessant touting of products that will bring us happiness, and the emerging social incivility and political antipathy of American politics, all of which are grounded in the belief that I am separate, indeed, better than those who differ from me. In contrast, Francis and Clare invite us to follow the humble Galilean, who gave up individualism that he might embrace the world.

I am profoundly moved by Clare's counsel to Agnes of Prague. In describing Jesus's incarnation and crucifixion, Clare provided a path to downward mobility:

> O most Noble Queen, gaze upon [Him],
> Consider [Him],
> Contemplate [Him],
> As you desire to imitate [Him].[24]

Clare found inspiration in gazing on the suffering Jesus of the cross. Fully identifying with Christ's suffering, Clare experienced the freedom of seeing herself as vulnerable and joined with the poor of the earth. As I gaze with Clare at Jesus's empathetic incarnation, I am reminded of the lines of another childhood hymn, "Nothing of my own I bring / Simply to the Cross I cling." In embracing the suffering of the world, in letting go of my privilege and wealth, I gain the world of grace. I experience the graceful interdependence of God. I discover that in losing my individualistic isolation, I gain everything, a life of companionship with God and God's creation.

To live simply is to put yourself at God's disposal, embodied in the persons God leads into your life. Simplicity is a lifestyle of openness to be in harmony and unity with others, lived out daily. We practice simplicity by listening to those around us rather than our own ego needs and personal gratification. By transcending individualism, we experience beloved community with those around us.

Abundance and Sacrifice

I'm an early riser, almost monastic in spirit as I waken between 4:00 a.m. and 5:00 a.m. each day to practice my morning rituals of contemplative prayer, study and writing, and walking on our local beach. I am probably more attached to my morning ritual than my retirement account or comfortable home. Recently, as I was happily writing and hoping to get to the beach, one of my grandchildren, who had spent the night with us, came quietly down the stairs and made a beeline toward me. My heart was with my grandson but my mind was with the next sentence I was writing—it just happened to be on holy simplicity! In that moment, I felt God's call to let go of my project to embrace my grandson. After half an hour of talking and reading with me, he

THE GIFTS OF DOWNWARD MOBILITY

decided he wanted to wake up his grandma. I returned to my work, inspired, having lost nothing from letting go of my agenda. This same reality is true when a stranger calls on my help or a person being bullied requires my support.

I have discovered that when I let go of my most precious possession, the ability to determine my time without the interference of others, I end up experiencing greater energy, insight, and creativity. My world expands beyond self-interest, opening me to God's wisdom and the inspiration that flows through me when I tear down the walls of ego and isolation.

The apostle Paul said that God's "grace is sufficient for me, for God's power is made perfect in weakness" (2 Corinthians 12:9, AP). We can experience divine abundance when we let go of possessiveness, sacrificing our time, talent, and treasures for the wellbeing of others.

Francis sought to be a fool for Christ, not a religious authority lording it over others with his spiritual practices and mystical experiences, but being with one with others in their common humanity and identity as God's beloved children. Francis and Clare even realized that their emphasis on poverty and simple living could be an impediment to their solidarity with others if they saw their evangelical lifestyle as a form of spiritual privilege, marking them as superior to their neighbors. Francis counseled one of his followers to give his Bible away to provide for the poor. What good is Scripture if you don't see God in the book of creation or the face of a hungry child?

Even our intelligence, political correctness, and moral certitude can isolate us from God's voice whispering through those around us. As a writer, professor, and pastor, I have been convicted of my intellectual pride on more than one occasion by the story of the professor and the monk. According to Buddhist wisdom, a renowned university professor visited a famous Zen master, desiring to know the secret of Zen Buddhism. While the master quietly served tea, the professor, exhibiting his intellectual acuity, talked about the principles of Zen. The master poured the visitor's cup to the brim, and then kept pouring. The professor watched the tea overflowing on the table until he could no longer restrain himself. "It's full! No more will go in!" the professor exclaimed. "This is you," the master replied. "How can I show you Zen unless you first empty your cup?" Intellectual prowess and moral purity can separate us from those we teach and counsel when we believe that our achievements are signs of superiority.

This same temptation to moral and intellectual superiority is surely at work in our current political and cultural incivility, whether in political diatribes or social media taunts. Inspired by binary divisions of right and wrong, us and them, we call those who differ from us "unpatriotic," "racist," "leftists," and "sexists," failing to see our common humanity beneath apparent difference. Often, I must resist the temptation to use my greater intelligence and access to information as a weapon against those I perceive as ignorant, uninformed, and lost in their fake news. I can stand for truth and for my personal beliefs and still affirm my solidarity as one fallible mortal in conversation with other fallible mortals.

As I noted earlier, the church needs to have a rummage sale every five hundred years to respond creatively to the challenges of the current age and jettison outmoded doctrines and traditions. Doctrinal orthodoxy, like ethical righteousness, can lead to judgment and alienation, which distance us from suffering and wayward humanity. In proclaiming our doctrinal and ethical superiority, we forget that we are also standing in need of grace and that saints are sinners, too! Theology is important, but theology without loving solidarity is a "noisy gong or a clanging symbol," simply a matter of graceless words, sound and fury signifying nothing.

The Politics of Simplicity

As people of privilege in terms of education, leisure, wealth, and political stability, how then shall we live? There is, after all, the hopelessness of the privileged who believe that, despite our privilege, we don't have the power or resources to change our lives or the world and that we are trapped in a system that prevents us from making any significant personal or political change. To people like ourselves, St. Elizabeth Seton advised, "Live simply so others can simply live." In response to our sense of hopelessness, Francis and Clare remind us that God is often found in subtraction rather acquisition and that abundant life comes from contentment, not control. Although Francis and Clare did not see themselves as political activists, their focus on holy poverty had political implications for both church and state. When the masses starve, how should a wealthy church respond? When peasants lose their property, what are the implications for the church, a large landowner in Francis's time? How does the opulent attire of prelates and priests reflect the One who counseled his followers to sell everything they have and give to the poor? How does consumerism and materialism, characteristic of our time, square with the daily experiences of landless peasants, hungry children, refugees escaping war, immigrants seeking asylum, and homeless persons living in the shadow of million-dollar homes? These questions provoke a serious examination of conscience for those who seek to follow the way of Jesus.

Simplifying our lives, embracing appropriate forms of spiritual downward mobility, is essential to the survival of countless animal species, the life-supporting ecosystem, and the future of generations to come. Simplicity of life is a matter of spiritual awareness, especially among people who have the leisure to study and travel. Our calling is to commit ourselves to spiritual and domestic decluttering, evident in daily practices of letting go of the cumber that destroys our souls and the lives of the poor.

At the very least, those of us in North America need to buy locally, consume less, turn down our thermostats, and find fuel-efficient ways to travel. This is a matter of personal choice. It is also a matter of political activism, especially when political leaders deny climate change and chant "drill, baby, drill" and install oil pipelines on sacred lands. In truth, the whole earth is sacred. There are "thin places" everywhere and simplicity of life awakens us to the holiness of each moment as well as every wave, bird, companion animal, and foot of soil. While we might not march with climate activists, we can care for Brother Air and Water, and Sister Right Whale and Monarch Butterfly by our lifestyle, phone calls, letters, and organizing. There is enough for our need—and our need must include the nonhuman world—but not for our greed. We must, as climate activist Bill McKibben asserts, recognize that the most important thing an individual can do to respond to climate change is quit being an individual. Simplicity is ultimately not about our individual choices but our willingness as persons in community to bless the earth and its inhabitants by seeing our common origins in divine creativity and common identity, human and nonhuman alike, as God's beloved children. As Francis and Clare discovered, the path of holy simplicity, of blessed poverty and spiritual downsizing, joins us with the way of Jesus, with the path to Calvary and new life as companions of the Risen One. God is in the least of these, and when we let go of every divisive wall, we are companions to the least of these as well.

IN THE SPIRIT OF ST. FRANCIS

Francis and Clare challenge us to live simply, letting go of all that stands between us and our neighbor, and us and God. The apparent subtraction, characteristic of simplicity of life, is, in fact, a process of addition in terms of joy, connection, and compassion.

Economic Examen

Mindfulness is essential to spiritual growth. Prayerful reflection on our values is often the first step to a changed lifestyle. For most Americans consumerism is the air we breathe. Most of us can't imagine a life without credit cards or immediate gratification on Amazon, Wayfair, and other online marketplaces. Deferred gratification and downward mobility go against the American way. In an economic examen, we look at our attitudes toward ownership and consumption. Like the Ignatian spiritual examen, we begin with silent awareness of God's presence, followed by a sense of gratitude for the blessings we've received and the graceful interdependence that sustains, nourishes, and inspires us. Grateful for the gift of life, take fifteen to twenty minutes each day over three or four days to look deeply at your life:

- What is your attitude toward money? Do you live by abundance or scarcity?
- What is your attitude toward your possessions? Are they the source of your happiness or do you find happiness elsewhere?
- During the past day or so, is there an event or experience that reflects your attitude toward finances, consumption, or ownership? How did this experience or event reflect your relationship with God and your spiritual values?
- In what ways are you possessed by your possessions?
- What helps you experience spiritual freedom in relationship to your possessions?

Ask for God's guidance in relating to your possessions, including finances and property, in ways that promote your own spiritual wellbeing and the wellbeing of those around you. Ask God to give you a generous spirit in the conduct of your economic life.

Spiritual Decluttering

When I was a pastor in western Maryland, I spent a good of time with the local apple farmers. One afternoon, I engaged a farmer in a conversation during pruning season in which I asked, "Why do you prune your apple trees?" With a wry smile, he responded, "To let the light in." Spiritual decluttering and downward mobility are practices aimed at simplifying our lives so that God's light can shine more fully in and through us. Many of us, as the Quakers counsel, are the victims of our own "cumber." Like the rich man in the gospel, we are possessed by our possessions.

Holy simplicity or spiritual decluttering involve a process of letting go of everything that stands between us and God. This may include letting go of our possessions, schedules, busyness, and intellectual superiority to feel solidarity with others, most particularly the vulnerable and poor. In living more simply, we make room for God to transform our lives. We experience the fabric of relationships that inspires us to identify our own wellbeing with the wellbeing of others. We learn with Mother Seton to "live simply so others might simply live."

Reflecting on your life, where do you need to simplify your life to be more attentive to God, those around you, and the wellbeing of the planet and its creatures? What areas of your life require spiritual pruning to let the light of God flow in and through your life more abundantly? Consider your:

- Finances
- Time
- Schedule
- Intellectual elitism
- Spiritual superiority
- Politics
- Relationships

Remember that as we seek God's realm above all, we will discover that we have everything we need to flourish and serve God and our neighbors.

Ultimate Concern

Theologian Paul Tillich described faith as involving our ultimate concern, or what is most important in our lives. Our ultimate concern promises ultimate fulfillment and asks for ultimate sacrifice. Many people see their ultimate concern in terms of success, consumption, power, family, health, and personal accomplishment. All these can be positive, provided they do not dominate their lives. For example, writing is an important part of my life. But if my writing prevents me from attending to my family and persons in need, it has become an idol harmful to myself and others. I must be willing to let go of my writing project to care for a sick grandchild. I need to put down the book I'm reading if my wife, grandchild, friend, or congregant need my emotional support. There are times in which service at the soup kitchen or going to a meeting in support of clean energy must take precedence over study and writing. I am a person of privilege and I need to use my privilege to claim my vocation as God's companion in healing the world.

In the spirit of the examen, ask God to reveal to you the nature of your ultimate concern, the values around which you construct your life. Does your ultimate concern join you with your loved ones? Does it promote solidarity with the poor and the nonhuman world? Does your ultimate concern draw you nearer to God's vision for your life? Does it give glory to God?

Ask for God's guidance in liberating you from the unnecessary so that you can experience God's presence in your life and in the world.

CHAPTER SIX

Holy Relationships

Set me as a seal upon your heart,
   as a seal upon your arm;
for love is strong as death,
   passion fierce as the grave.
Its flashes are flashes of fire,
   a raging flame.
Many waters cannot quench love,
   neither can floods drown it.
If one offered for love
   all the wealth of one's house,
   it would be utterly scorned.

(Song of Solomon 8:6-7)

Early on in our relationship, my wife, Kate, introduced me to her spiritual mentor, United Church of Christ pastor, spiritual guide, and political activist Allan Armstrong Hunter. In the course of getting to know Hunter, I was impressed when I heard that although Hunter had been happily married for nearly fifty years, he and a female spiritual friend covenanted over many years to pray for each other at the same time every day. Their spiritual friendship deepened their faith and added zest to their personal and professional relationships.

These days, many persons have been inspired by the wisdom of Celtic spirituality. Celtic Christians described certain relationships by the word *anamcara,* or friend of the soul. These special spiritual relationships were characterized by their spiritual intimacy and mutual spiritual guidance. Alienation and individualism were overcome in the common quest to experience the holiness of one another as embodiments of God's loving wisdom and creativity. In the spirit of the Celtic affirmation of "thin places" where heaven and earth were transparent to one another, these spiritual relationships were "thin" in their imparting of divinity to flesh and blood, spiritual adventures, and faithful and committed human relationships. While such spiritual friendships may be rare and must be conducted with the highest ethical standards, many of us experience God's presence in our own spiritual journeys through egalitarian spiritual relationships as well as professional relationships with spiritual guides or directors, who remind us that we are always on holy ground and that God's presence is our deepest reality.

Clare and Francis came into each other's life when Clare was in her teens and Francis his late twenties. Like Francis, Clare Offreduccio (1193-1253) was a child of wealth and privilege. She was also a child of divine destiny. During her pregnancy, Clare's deeply spiritual mother received a prophecy that God would be with her, protecting her unborn child and prophesying that she would be a light to the world. In response, she chose the name Chiara, "luminous," for her daughter. Clare had every educational, social, and recreational advantage available to a young person in her time. Her future was planned for her: She would marry someone from her noble class and live comfortably, carrying on the family line. Yet, Clare walked to the beat of a different drum and sought another kind of family rather than that of her biological origins. From the very beginning, Clare inclined toward the Spirit, dedicating much of her childhood to prayerful contemplation. Although many nobles sought her hand in marriage, she confessed that she was looking for a truly exceptional suitor, one who would fulfill her spiritual desires. For her, the ideal suitor was God's beloved son, Jesus of Nazareth.

When Clare first heard Francis speak, she discovered what she had been looking for: a life of spiritual commitment and simplicity, devoted fully to God. A spark ignited between the noble Clare and the itinerant friar, who had forsaken the dream of nobility for the way of Jesus, and Clare and Francis began to meet privately to reflect on the spiritual life and Clare's calling into the monastic life. Francis was her teacher and she was, in her own words, his "little spiritual plant." But she was more than just Francis's protégé. Clare experienced the call to spiritual adventure, to embody women's spirituality and reflect the image of God in her life and in the lives of those whom she would touch.

On Palm Sunday 1212, Clare abandoned her comfortable lifestyle to follow the path of Franciscan simplicity and God-intoxication. Like Francis, she was met with anger from her father and relatives, who attempted forcefully to bring her home. Clinging to the altar, Clare protested, proclaiming that her from now on her husband would be Jesus. Her family relented when she took off her veil, revealing her closely cropped hair.

Francis was initially Clare's spiritual mentor and she placed her spiritual life in his hands. Yet, in truly deep relationships, hierarchical roles are eventually replaced by a democracy of the Spirit. God had given Clare a mind of her own and she envisioned a women's monastic order, complementary to Francis's emerging order, that would be led by women who established, contrary to custom, their own Rule or practices to follow. Though tethered to one spot due to spiritual convention and safety concerns for women, the Poor Ladies or Poor Clares created a monastery at San Damiano, outside of Assisi. Cloistered and devoted to simplicity and the vision of poverty Francis and Clare shared, they ensured that San Damiano would be a place of hospitality where all are pilgrims and none are strangers. They often provided hospitality to pilgrims, lepers, and persons experiencing economic duress. Residing where Francis received his calling to rebuild the church, Clare would create her own structures of spiritual transformation, awakening women to their calling as God's beloved daughters, bearing the image of God. This was extraordinary in a society and church that regarded women as "occasions of sin," inferior to their male counterparts. One biographer of Clare notes both truthfully and sadly that "she succeeded in becoming holy *in spite of* being a woman."[25]

Clare and Francis were deep spiritual friends. Francis reached out to Clare when he sought guidance about the future of his mission: Would he retreat to the quiet of monastic life or immerse himself in the maelstrom of public preaching? After much prayer, Clare counseled Francis that his vocation called him to go out into the world and preach the Gospel.

Francis and Clare met rarely in their fifteen-year relationship, although it is possible that they communicated through messengers. Perhaps, they realized their deep spiritual passion for one another and wished to maintain their relationship on a spiritual plane. Nevertheless, Francis and Clare had one memorable meeting. At Clare's urging they met for a repast, surrounded by male and female companions. Deeply engaged in spiritual conversation, Clare and Francis barely touched their meal. But their meeting soon roused the concern of neighboring villagers, who saw a fiery light emanating from the woods and assumed that a brush fire had started. Instead, what appeared to a forest fire mirrored the passion of their love for God and one another. Some suggest, in the spirit of Carl Jung, that Francis and Clare completed each other spiritually in their joining of *animus*, masculine, and *anima*, feminine, aspects of creation and human existence. As one scholar notes:

> In meeting Clare, Francis found the feminine side of himself, his tenderness, and in that relationship with Francis, Clare found the masculine side of herself, her strength. Each of them chased fear away from the other. Francis no longer had any fear of becoming tender and thus became strong. Clare, through her relationship with Francis, developed her own tenderness and thus became strong. Francis rediscovered his masculinity in Clare, his strength, and Clare found her femininity in Francis, her nourishment, her tenderness.[26]

Transcending stereotypes of masculinity and femininity and gender roles, our spiritual relationships enable us to grow in wisdom and stature as Jesus did, and embrace activity and receptivity, power and compassion, relationship and solitude, emotion and intellect. Holy relatedness awakens us to the energy of love that radiates from our holy friendships to embrace the whole earth with tender strength. In prayerfully engaging in personal or professional spiritual relationships, we experience God incarnate in our domestic lives and daily spiritual adventures.

Clare once had a vision in which she brought a basin of water with a towel to dry Francis's hands. As she grew nearer, Francis bared his chest and invited her to nurse from his breast. Perhaps Clare's vision reveals not only the interplay of Francis's and Clare's integration of the masculine and feminine, but also of Francis's role in Clare's spiritual nourishment. His nurture may have enabled Clare to embrace the masculine aspects of life, enabling her to confront ecclesiastical attempts to dominate her order. Yet, Clare did not seek to imitate Francis, but Francis's "little spiritual plant" grew to uniquely embody Christ, whose love joined them in spirit and mission. Clare gazed upon Jesus, seeking to live a Christ-filled and cross-centered life, giving up privilege and comfort to share in Jesus's suffering on behalf of humankind.

Francis and Clare provide a model for holistic spiritual relationships. Christ is the *anamcara* of all creation, who mirrors to us our divine origin and destiny. In Christ's mirroring, we discover our identity as God's beloved children regardless of age, gender, sexual identity, ethnicity, race, or giftedness. In placing our most passionate spiritual relationships in the light of Christ, we make a commitment to making these relationships whole and holy and avoid the complications of sexual passion if we already are in committed relationships. The fires of the Spirit embrace the whole person, body, mind, spirit, relationships, and citizenship, and require us to create boundaries of love that support our vocation as God's companions in healing the world, whether this involves our family, community, church, or planet.

In the Spirit of St. Francis

Holy relationships inspire spiritual transformation and take us from self-interest to world loyalty. Love, as Plato says, enables us to grow wings and gives us the wisdom to experience eternal Beauty within the beauty of our world. An anchor spiritual passage in my own spiritual life and this text is Dag Hammarskjöld's affirmation:

> For all that has been—thanks!
> For all that shall be—yes![27]

I invoked this passage earlier in the text as an inspiration to give thanks for God's blessings in our lives and the gifts of our good earth as well as to awaken us to our future as followers in the way of Jesus. Gratitude, affirmation, and possibility also shape our understanding of *anamcara* or spiritual friendship. I have been blessed to have had a spiritual friend and to share spiritual values with my wife, Kate.

Giving Thanks for Friendship

After a time of stillness, begin a period of gratitude—for the gift of life, for the wonder of your personal life as a reflection of divine wisdom and creativity, for those who have loved you, and for the beauty and nurture of the earth. Then, narrow down your gratitude to focus on friendships that have nurtured your spirit. You may choose to consider the following questions as a prompt for reflection:

- Who were my closest friends as a child? What was special about them? What aspects of the relationship do I carry with me today?
- Who were my closest friends as a youth? What was special about them? What aspects of the relationship do I carry with me today?

- What have been my most meaningful relationships in adulthood? Were any of these relationships spiritual in nature? Could any of these be described in terms of the word *anamcara* "friend of the soul?" How did these relationships deepen my relationship with God? Do I have any spiritual relationships that currently deepen my relationship with God?

Our deepest relationships call us to gratitude. Take some time to give thanks for these unique and spiritually nurturing relationships.

Awakening to Spiritual Friendships

The gift of relationships invites us to share in the great yes of God's presence in our lives and those around us. As you look at your life and relationships, are there persons with whom you feel a spiritual connection yet unexplored? Are there persons for whom you might be a mentor or spiritual guide? Are there persons who might benefit from your counsel and personal witness?

The great yes may also involve deepening your spiritual relationship with those persons you encounter daily, in particular, spouses and life partners, parents, children, siblings, friends, coworkers. Ask for God's guidance in discerning ways you can creatively inject greater spirituality in your relationships. The nature of this spiritual focus often differs depending on the relationship. With my grandchildren, it may mean more closely observing what is important to them, their fears and joys, their imaginations, their dreams. It likely means listening with the heart for God's deepest desires for them and intentionally responding to nurture these desires. With my wife, it also means listening to what is spoken and unspoken and going beyond habitual behaviors and the lenses through which I view our relationship. It may mean listening more deeply to God's deepest desires for them and intentionally responding to these desires in word, action, and attitude.

If you do not have a close spiritual friendship, a friendship that enables you to draw closer to God's vision for your life, you may choose to establish a relationship with a professional spiritual director or friend. To find a friend that speaks to your spirit, you may want to contact your priest, pastor, imam, or rabbi for a referral, contact a center in your locale where persons study to become spiritual directors, or contact a professional agency such as Spiritual Directors International.

From Self-Interest to World Loyalty

Then Jesus told his disciples, "If any want to become my followers, let them deny themselves and take up their cross and follow me. For those who want to save their life will lose it, and those who lose their life for my sake will find it. For what will it profit them if they gain the whole world and forfeit their life? Or what will they give in return for their life?"

(Matthew 16:24-26)

Salvation, whether described as this-worldly personal whole-ness or everlasting life, can be experienced in many ways. In the church of my childhood, the road to salvation involved making a public confession of Jesus as your personal savior and then knowing you would go to heaven when you died. For some religious traditions, salvation involves participation in the sacra-ments and rituals of their church. For still others, it is looking for the signs of the end times and counting the days till the Second Coming of Jesus, when the earth will be destroyed and the saved are lifted up to heaven. In these versions of salvation, everlasting life involves a type of divine rescue operation delivering us from the evils of this world, or a privileged heavenly status in which those who believe the right things are saved while the rest of the world goes to hell. Salvation is, then, a type of spiritual transaction which places me in an elite status others will not achieve.

Individualistic heavenly privilege, reflected in the binary separation of saved and unsaved, believer and unbeliever, are paramount in binary versions of salvation. These otherworldly concepts of salvation tragically diminish our sense of connection with our fellow humans and add to the binary divisiveness of the world. If someone falls outside the true faith, they are lesser mortals, even children of the devil, who deserve little or no ethical or legal consideration. With heaven as your destination, there is no reason to care for the fate of the earth and millions of nonhuman species.

Francis of Assisi affirmed another kind of salvation, one that embraces, unites, and heals the world and affirms God's loving faithfulness in the next. In the world of praise described in Francis's "Canticle of the Creatures," the saint describes God's love as all-embracing, including the human and nonhuman world. Going beyond the binary "in" and "out" understandings of salvation, Francis saw salvation as involving ever-expanding circles of divine and human love and connectedness with all creation. In speaking of Francis's spiritual journey, early biographer Thomas of Celano described Francis's life as moving from the practice of prayer to becoming prayer itself. The ultimate practice of connection, prayer breaks down the barriers between God and us, so that even in our fallibility, we can discover that we are one in spirit with God and our neighbor.

Eight centuries later, Thomas Merton had a similar experience of experiencing life as one great prayer while walking the streets of Louisville, Kentucky, on an outing from the Trappist monastery in Gethsemani, Kentucky.

At the corner of Fourth and Walnut, in the center of the
shopping district, I was suddenly overwhelmed with the
realization that I loved all those people, that they were
mine and I was theirs, that we could not be alien to one
another even though we were total strangers. It was like
waking from a dream of separateness.... The whole illusion of separate holy existence is a dream.[28]

Merton discovered that there is no "other" as our souls expand
to embrace the universe in its wondrous beauty and tragedy. The
walls of isolation collapse and we are joined with the joy and
sorrow of all creation. We experience God in all things and all
things in God as the divine energy of love flows in and though us
to all creation.

Following the spirit of Francis, many of us today prayerfully
chant the words, "My God and all things!" God and the world
are one. Personal identity is real, our uniqueness matters and is to
be honored, but our self is grounded in God's Self and God's Self
is our deepest, most dynamic identity. We have discovered that
faith in God joins us with all creation as companions and healers.
Trusting God with eternity, we experience salvation in the holy
here and now. Salvation and everlasting life are this-worldly experiences arising as a result of embrace and inclusion rather than
individualism.

At the heart of the Franciscan vision is the journey from individualistic self-interest to spiritual self-centeredness, when
self and God are in sync, to world loyalty. Philippians 2:5-11
describes Christ's kenotic selfhood and asserts that this same self-
emptying, world-embracing spirit is our destiny as well. God is, as

Bonaventure and Nicolas of Cusa asserted, a circle whose center is everywhere and whose circumference is nowhere. The finite experiences we treasure reflect divine love, but our individual experiences lean toward a greater Selfhood.

Sadly, most of the time we see ourselves primarily as isolated, individual selves, standing out and separated, only casually related to the joys and the sorrows of the world. Individualistic selfhood focuses only on what I perceive to be my isolated, individualistic, self-made personality. From this perspective, self-interest in terms of power, wealth, and celebrity is the highest good. But such self-interest is fragile and ultimately fails to bring happiness. Whether in terms of rugged individualism or policies that exalt national individualism, security is bought at the price of constant vigilance and defensiveness. Everyone is a potential competitor and adversary. Only the strong and independent survive, while the vulnerable are condemned to hopelessness and neglect.

Franciscan spirituality asserts that the independent, isolated self, or ego, is an illusion. We cannot go it alone. Everything we achieve is grounded in our relationships to those who give us life and nurture us, to the universe, and to the ever-creative and ever-inspiring God. As Martin Luther King, Jr., wisely noted, we are bound together in an intricate garment of destiny in which "I cannot be what I ought to be until you are what you ought to be. And you can never be what you ought to be until I am what I ought to be."[29]

Francis's "Canticle of the Creatures" described his experience of a world of praise in which each creature is an essential contributor to the divine symphony. Francis's canticle of praise describes in poetic terms the intricate and interdependent Body of Christ, encompassing personal identity, the church, and the world, affirmed by the apostle Paul:

> For just as the body is one and has many members, and all the members of the body, though many, are one body, so it is with Christ.... But God has so arranged the body, giving the greater honor to the inferior member, that there may be no dissension within the body, but the members may have the same care for one another. If one member suffers, all suffer together with it; if one member is honored, all rejoice together with it. Now you are the body of Christ and individually members of it.
> (I Corinthians 12:13, 24-27)

While Paul may initially have meant the spirit of the early Christian community as the mystical body of Christ, clearly the body of Christ goes well beyond the institutional church to embrace the universe. Like the intricate interplay of body, mind, and spirit, divine energy flows through every part of the person, enlivening and inspiring part and whole seamlessly. As Paul asserts in Romans 8, the groanings of the nonhuman world are intimately connected with our own quest for wholeness. The Spirit speaking in our lives in sighs too deep for words is also moving through the woodlands, streams, oceans, flora, fauna, and every creature. In a time of global climate change, we are challenged to recognize that there is no isolated individual or nation, for we are all bound together in a single destiny.

Francis would have been at home with Anglo-American philosopher Alfred North Whitehead's assertion that religion evolves from the worship of power and fear of God to the amazement at God's loving creativity, inspiring us to imitate our Creator. He writes, "The new, and almost profane, concept of the goodness of God replaces the older emphasis on the will of God.... You study [God's] goodness in order to be like [God]."[30] From this perspective, divine and human perfection reflect all-embracing love rather than isolated independence. Divine and human power are manifest in solidarity with the joys and sufferings of others. Fulfillment and peace of mind are found in the kenotic self-emptying that inspired Francis and Clare. Authentic peace is experienced when we see others' well-being as essential to our own. Walls are torn down and bridges built with humanity and creation in all its diversity. Without the need to defend or protect, life in all its diversity and contrast becomes a gift, shaping my experience and enabling me to share my gifts with the world.

In an interdependent universe, wholeness emerges from experiencing our common origins and destinies. The ninety-nine sheep safely in the fold are incomplete and cannot experience authentic wellbeing without the wayward sheep finding its way home. Once again, in the words of Whitehead, authentic peace comes through empathy that gives birth to ever wider circles of compassion and care: "Peace is self-control at its widest—at the 'width' where the self has been lost and interest has been transferred to coordinations wider than personality."[31]

An ancient legend describes the adventures of a pilgrim and his beloved canine companion. For over a decade, they sojourned together, experiencing the wonder and tragedy of life, partners in a holy adventure. It so happened that both the pilgrim and his dog died on the same evening. The pilgrim himself, still in companionship with his canine companion at the gates of heaven, was told that he could gain entry, but that he must abandon his dog. Without blinking an eye, the pilgrim responded, "I will not enter heaven without my faithful companion. He has been faithful to me through thick and thin. We are not complete without each other. He will grieve if I abandon him." The heavenly gatekeeper responded joyfully, "You have passed the final test. You and your companion may enter heaven, for love is key!"

As the Lord's Prayer reveals, our calling is to be companions in God's realm "on earth as it is in heaven." If God is present in our lives and the world, we are already in heaven, we just don't know it. Heaven is found in our joyful embrace of one another, bound together by the love that brought us into life, that spun the galaxies, and propels the stars.

True self-centeredness involves going beyond isolating individuality to experience our centering in God and all things. The center is here and everywhere. World loyalty, grounded in the interdependence of life, compels us to care for the earth and its creatures. Others' suffering is my suffering. Others' celebration is my joy. While the future is shaped by those who pray for the world, our prayers may inspire us to protest, political involvement, and direct service to heal God's world. Mystics become activists when they recognize that we are all connected and that spiritual maturity involves the wellbeing of all of us and not just my personal, cloistered ecstasy. While there is no blueprint for world loyalty, surely the realities of climate change, poverty, refugees, pandemic, and injustice based on race, nationality, gender, and sexual identity inspire us to become God's companions in saving the world one act at a time, whether our actions involve standing by a Muslim woman harassed at the filling station, tutoring a vulnerable child at a neighborhood school, marching for justice and environmental healing, or picking up the phone and prayerfully telling your representatives or the White House to put persons ahead of profits, promote programs to end poverty, or challenge the relaxation of environmental protections.

Francis's life became a canticle of creation, a prayerful symphony of healing, in which every creature revealed God's grace and invited us to companionship and healing. This is our calling, to prayerfully breathe and walk, embracing beauty all around us and finding our identity as God's fellow musicians playing our role in a glorious symphony of praise and healing.

IN THE SPIRIT OF ST. FRANCIS

Francis experienced the world as one great prayer. Each of us, joined with one another, plays our role in bringing beauty to the world. Inspired by the canticle of all creation, we discover that we are part of one Great Breath, enlivening and enlightening all things. Healing emerges when every breath becomes a prayer and we move from individualistic isolation to interdependent world loyalty.

Breathe through Us, Breath of God

In this exercise, find a comfortable place to sit. Gaze at your environment, noting the unique beauty of your surroundings and your connection with the world around you. You may choose to close your eyes or pray with your eyes open. In the spirit of an earlier spiritual practice, begin by focusing on your breath, letting your breathing center your experience. As you inhale, experience God's energy of love filling your body from head to toe, healing every cell and awakening your soul to the wondrous unity of creation. Experience the profound giftedness of life and your dependence on

God's world for each breath. Exhale gently and calmly, returning your breath to the world in a healing way.

After a few minutes of opening to God's presence in your body, mind, and spirit, begin to focus equally on exhaling. See each exhalation as connecting you with all creation. Let each exhaling breath be your gift to the universe, beginning with your immediate environment and continuing in circles of love to your loved ones, religious organization, community, state, nation, and planet. Experience your peace radiating across the planet and into outer space. Feel your life as part of one Great Breath, flowing in and through you, as part of God's good earth. Let this divine breath energize and connect you with the wellsprings of creation, God's energy of love, and your fellow creatures.

As you conclude this exercise, let your intention be twofold: (1) to constantly experience life as a Great Breath and Prayer flowing in and through you, joining you with all creation, including those whose behaviors and politics repulse you, for they, too, are part of this Great Breath, and (2) to be open to where God calls you to use your gifts to bring wholeness to those around you, whether through personal relationships or personal involvement. Ask God to give you a sense of how you might live out your world loyalty and what you might do to bring justice and beauty to the earth. Keep your eyes open throughout the week, attentive to moments of guidance, inspiration, and action. God will show you the way to move from self-interest to world loyalty.

In conclusion, let your prayer be:

Breathe on us, breath of God,
fill us, inspire us, connect us, heal us.

Let every breath I take be a prayer of healing unity.
Let your energy of love fill me completely
that my life will be consecrated to you
one thought, word, and act at a time.
Amen.

CHAPTER EIGHT

Healing Circles

At Gubbio there was a woman with hands so crippled
that she was unable to handle anything with them. When
she heard that Saint Francis had entered the city she
immediately ran to him. With a sad and mournful face,
she showed him her crippled hands and begged him to
touch them. He was moved with great pity. He touched
her hands and healed them. The woman returned home,
full of joy, made a cheesecake with her hands and offered
it to the holy man.[32]

No one believed that young Stephen had a future. Nine years
old, this Northern California boy experienced crippling
seizures, often without warning. No end was in sight except a
life of dependence on others. Physicians and teachers believed he
would never be able to drive a car, go to college, or raise a family.
Some speculated that he would be intellectually disabled as well as
a result of recurring seizures that rendered him unconscious and
often led to hospital visits. Hoping against hope, one Saturday
afternoon, his parents took him to a healing service at a local
church in his community. The presiding minister placed the palms
of his hands on Stephen's forehead, prayed with conviction, and
then anointed him with oil. Nothing dramatic happened at the
time. In fact, nothing happened at all for several days. They kept

waiting for a return to his former condition but there were no more seizures. His physician confirmed that something amazing and unaccountable had happened. Stephen was cured. Nobody could explain the cure, except that it had resulted from the touch of the Master's hand, the power of God to heal the sick, restore the broken, welcome the lost, and transform cells as well as souls. Healed through God's grace, this nine-year-old boy decided that would become a physician and later a seminary-educated medical missionary. Touched by God, he has spent his lifetime sharing God's love through prayerful medicine in the United States and across the globe.

The Healing Power of Faith

Shrouded in legend, and often appearing to be a replication of accounts of Jesus's healing ministry, Francis's healing ministry been downplayed by priests, scholars, and laypersons alike. Like other hagiographical stories, early accounts of Francis's life reveal him not only to be an ecclesiastical reformer, nature mystic, spiritual teacher, justice seeker, and movement founder, but also describe him as a thirteenth-century embodiment of Jesus's healing ministry.

During his lifetime, Francis employed healing techniques as diverse as prayerful touch and laying on of hands, prayer, the sign of the cross, and exorcism in response to ailments such as physical disfigurement, paralysis, epilepsy, and demonic possession. After Francis's death, persons experienced healings as a result of their prayers to the saint, touching his coffin, sleeping in his tomb, and dreams in which Francis appeared as a healing presence.

While nineteenth- and twentieth-century theologians and biblical scholars considered the healing of Jesus and his saintly followers as relics of a bygone era, reflecting the superstitions of a prescientific age, today we are discovering that prayer, faith, and religious commitment can be factors in prevention and recovery from illness, emotional health, stress reduction, and overall physical wellbeing. In everyday life, spontaneous healings occur, sometimes as a result of prayer and other times for no observable reason. Science is studying the sacred, and studies on the power of prayer and healing touch have led physicians to assert "prayer is good medicine" and "faith is good for your health."[33] Miraculous changes can occur in our lives and those for whom we pray, grounded in the healing powers of nature and the creative and loving wisdom of God.

Circles of Healing

Francis's affirmation that mysticism leads to activism is at the heart of this book. Mystical experiences transform our spirits, lifting us beyond everyday realities and giving us new perspectives, values, and purposes. The mystic's call is vocational, inspiring and enabling persons to participate in bringing God's realm "on earth as it is in heaven."

God's realm of Shalom embraces our spiritual lives. It also inspires ever-widening circles of love and healing, empowering persons to live out Jesus's mission to bring abundant life to wayward, struggling, and vulnerable humanity.

Jesus's ministry encompassed the totality of life, ranging from spiritual well-being to social healing. God's circle of love includes everyone, changing cells and social structures, welcoming outcasts, and challenging religious leaders. In his mission statement, echoing the prophet Isaiah, Jesus proclaimed:

The Spirit of the Lord is upon me,
  because he has anointed me
    to bring good news to the poor.
He has sent me to proclaim release to the captives
  and recovery of sight to the blind,
    to let the oppressed go free,
to proclaim the year of the Lord's favor.
(Luke 4:18-19)

While we can never fully describe or replicate the mechanics of Jesus's healing ministry, Jesus's focus was all-inclusive. No ailment was too large or small for Jesus to address. Holistic in nature, Jesus's healings changed peoples' social standing as well as their physical condition. Jesus brought the energy of love, residing in the big bang and the evolution of galaxies and planets, to address human suffering in its many forms. Rather than hoarding his healing power, Jesus promised his followers that, empowered by God's Spirit, they could do even greater things (see John 14:12).

Francis followed Jesus's counsel to live simply and give his possessions to the poor. Following Jesus, Francis also challenged anything that prevented people from experiencing the joy God intended for humankind. If the glory of God is a fully alive human, then every act of healing, whether physical, spiritual, relational, economic, political, or environmental, gives witness to God's glory and is mandated by Jesus, our Savior and Healer.

Reimagining Healing
Growing up in the Salinas Valley, California, I recall that every Sunday afternoon, my mother tuned into faith healers Oral Roberts and Kathryn Kuhlman. I still recall Oral Roberts, with

sweat pouring from his brow, slapping people on their foreheads and yelling, "Be healed," and Kathryn Kuhlman in her diaphanous gown purring, "I believe in miracles." They told stories of paralysis cured, sight recovered, and hearing restored. As a child, I found their antics hilarious but also confusing. I also wondered why some people were cured and others remained mired in pain and debilitation. Did God choose some and not others? Or did healing depend entirely on their faith? Despite the connection preachers made between faith and healing, I witnessed people with great faith dying of cancer and loving parents killed in automobile accidents.

Decades have passed since those Sunday afternoons of my childhood. But the impact of Roberts and Kuhlman still lingers. In my thirties, I rediscovered the healings of Jesus through an encounter with Jerry Jampolsky's attitudinal healing. I learned techniques of holistic medicine and became a practitioner and later teacher-master of Reiki healing touch, a type of energy work aimed at balancing and enhancing the healing energy of the universe as it flows through our lives.[34] I reclaimed the power of prayer as a way of awakening to God's ever-present energy of love, reflecting the deeper laws of nature often hidden from those who see only the surface of life. I came to believe that prayer reflected the intricate and graceful interdependence of life, connecting me with those for whom I prayed and opening persons to greater manifestations of God's loving energy. More than thirty years of joining intercessory prayer, healing worship, and Reiki healing touch has enabled me to reimagine Jesus's healing ministry as channeling the infinite energy of the universe, the energy of God's love, to comfort the vulnerable and transform finite human suffering. Through my involvement in Reiki healing touch, prayer, and liturgical healing, I have witnessed pain relief, stress reduction, emotional healing, the healing of memories, and peaceful dying. In the spirit of Jesus and his follower Francis, I believe that I am called to share in Jesus's path of healing in responding to pain wherever I encounter it, whether the result of physical, spiritual, relational, emotional, or social and political disease and disorder.

I believe that Francis can guide us toward a truly holistic approach to healing and wholeness. Although his activism was primarily interpersonal, Francis's expanded the circle of healing beyond the purely spiritual and physical to embrace economics and relationships. When Francis hugged the man afflicted with leprosy, the former outcast became part of a welcoming and gracious healing circle. While it is unclear that any of the persons with leprosy that Francis encountered received a physical healing, Francis, like Jesus before him, transformed lepers' self-understanding and social status. In hugging the lepers and visiting their communities, acting as if he were one of them, Francis called forth the image God that had been hidden by their disfigurement. In seeing persons with leprosy through the eyes of God's love, Francis awakened their own self-affirmation and challenged others to see them as God's beloved children.

The judgment of others often contracts our emotional lives. We see ourselves in terms of others' prejudice, fear, and hate. But when we are loved, we discover that we are somebody. We see ourselves as God sees us, holy and unique and capable of making a difference. We are God's children, loved and valuable, gifted and called, regardless of what the world says.

In hugging the disparaged and marginalized lepers, Francis transformed their social status. Just as Jesus's welcome of tax collectors, foreigners, and persons with illnesses that rendered them spiritually unclean restored them to the larger community, Francis's embrace of lepers told the world that illness cannot separate us from God's love, meaningful vocation, and our rightful place in the social order. If Francis and Jesus loved the sinful, sick, and segregated, then religious institutions and the social order must learn to love and welcome them as well. They must break down the walls of otherness and embrace the marginalized and broken as full members of the body of Christ. The body is the temple of God's spirit, a shrine of divinity, and that applies to everyone's body, regardless of its apparent disfigurement or deviation from social standards.

Franciscan healing is always personal and intimate as well as communal and global. Francis counseled his followers to seek their own spiritual healing through humility, simplicity, and identification with Jesus as their spiritual companion and guide. He challenged any limits to our care for the "others" in our midst. Following Jesus meant that no one was off limits in terms of our personal care and ethical consideration.

Francis recognized the importance of faithful communities for our holistic spiritual wellbeing. Franciscan communities presented an alternative vision of reality to that of the powerful and wealthy, including the affluent and powerful world of the church and its hierarchy, in their emphasis on poverty as well as their challenge to materialism and consumerism. These communities implicitly critiqued the social and political order of Francis's time by placing the spiritual above the material and prizing human and creaturely wellbeing above status, power, and wealth. In following Francis today, we must chart expanding circles of hospitality and welcome, with special concern for those who have been forgotten and, tragically, persecuted by church and society.

Prophetic Healing

Francis advocated what I describe as prophetic healing, a lifestyle and politics of healing that overcomes polarization and incivility. Healthy communities nurture spiritually and physically healthy persons and families. While we can choose poverty as part of our spiritual discipline, we recognize that involuntary poverty disempowers and diminishes. Theologian and spiritual guide Howard Thurman asserted that one of the primary costs of poverty and prejudice is that it stifles children's imaginations. Meant to soar to the heavens, they are embedded in the realities of day to day survival. Yet, the divine energies within all persons call the impoverished and oppressed to claim God's vision for themselves and the world.

Francis recognized his own economic and social privilege and relinquished that privilege by following the path of simplicity and hospitality. Frugal himself, he recognized that communities needed to be generous to the least of these and ultimately that requires changes in their policies and practices to promote healing and wholeness. Like Martin Luther King, Jr., and Mahatma Gandhi centuries later, Francis believed spiritual transformation was possible for oppressor and oppressed alike: While the forgotten and marginalized need to be lifted up and challenged to be agents in their destiny, the wealthy and powerful need to be challenged to let go of the perquisites of wealth and status and to be open to God's presence in the poor as well as in their own lives. The spiritual arc of history, God's aim at wholeness for our planet, flows through all of us, inviting us to share in God's dream of shalom.

Francis focused on the healing of humankind's relationship with the nonhuman world. While contemporary issues of ecology and climate change would have been foreign to him, his vision of a world of praise inspires compassionate care for the nonhuman world that in our time inspires policies that promote environmental justice. The holiness of the nonhuman world, reflected in creatures' ability to praise God, promotes ethical consideration for the nonhuman world as well as the recognition that we—and all creatures—are in this together. Realizing God's dream of shalom takes us beyond humankind to become God's partners in healing the earth. We cannot find personal healing if the planet is dying. A healed planet nurtures healed persons and unleashes spiritual possibilities in all of us.

In the Spirit of St. Francis

Franciscan healing calls us to be healers too! Each moment can be a healing moment when people draw near to God through praise, gratitude, generosity, repentance, and service. You can tip the balance from sickness to health, from death to life, by your prayers and acts of kindness. Your care for others may effect changes in body, mind, and spirit—and even the political and economic order. The questions Francis's healing ministry raises for us as citizens and individuals in community are: Do you want to be healed? What are you willing to sacrifice and embrace to experience healing? Do you want your community and nation to be healed? What are you willing to do to achieve civic healing? Do you want the planet to be healed? What sacrifices will you make to go from consumerism to simplicity?

Blessing the World

Francis and his companions were known to greet people with "God's peace to you." Peace is just a moment away when we turn to God in gratitude and then share our gifts with others. In the spirit of Francis, I have begun a version of Francis's greeting, most of the time as a silent spiritual practice, but often in relational encounters. I begin the day with the affirmation: "I bless everyone I meet." During my sunrise walk on a nearby beach, I silently bless other walkers and the occupant of cars going by. I pause to bless persons I see on the news, including politicians whose policies and behaviors I find deplorable. At the end of conversations with friends and strangers, I often say, "Bless you." I believe a life of blessing tips the balance toward healing and reminds me I can bring healing to every encounter.

In the days ahead, choose to become a person of blessing, invoking God's blessing and peace in every encounter as you align your spirit and words with people you meet.

Listening to Your Life

Author Frederick Buechner advises us to listen to our lives to discern the movements of grace and blessing that flow to and through our joys and challenges. Francis would agree that self-awareness and God-awareness are connected. When we listen to our lives, we discover where we need healing and how we can participate as God's companions in healing the world, one person and practice at a time. We experience our own holiness as God's beloved children. The art of listening to our experiences and encounters enables us to discern how best to respond to political and social issues. When we listen to God's Spirit whispering in sighs too deep for words, we see the holiness in others and often we discern the most compassionate and effective way to respond in a non-polarizing but courageous way to heal, challenge, and transform the machinations of the powers and principalities into systems that support personal and planetary wellbeing.

First, we begin with our own healing. After a time of meditative silence, ask God to reveal to you places where you need God's healing touch. Where do you feel broken, anxious, diseased, and alienated in body, mind, spirit, and relationships? How does this shape your responses and behaviors? In what ways does this limit you? In what ways and with whom might you find greater healing in response to these places of brokenness and pain?

Then, in meditative prayer, ask God's peace to descend on you, restoring you to wholeness. Even when problems persist and you continue to deal with physical ailments, you may discover that even when a cure is deferred or not apparently possible, there can be a healing. Ask God to help you discover that God's grace is sufficient for you and that God's power is made perfect in weakness and solidarity with others. You may also choose to ask God for solutions in terms of changed behaviors, lifestyle, or persons who can support your healing process.

Through it all, give thanks for the gift of love and life, remembering that nothing in all creation can separate you from the love of God.

Letting Your Life Speak

Out of your own quest for healing comes the inspiration and guidance to heal the world, locally and globally. Each act of kindness contributes to the healing of the planet. Kindness of spirit takes many forms: a direct but civil call to our political representatives regarding policy decisions related to immigrants, gun safety, health care, climate change, or equal rights; volunteering at a soup kitchen, house raising, or environmental cleanup; picketing and protesting an injustice in a matter that encourages conversation; reaching out to people who hold contrasting political positions in a civil and caring fashion, looking for common good; praying for political leaders, despite your concerns for their policies.

We can raise our voices for peace and healing in terms of individual relationships and political decisions. We need a healed planet to be fully healed persons. We can pray, "Lord, make me an instrument of your peace," as we challenge policies that make for war, oppression, and poverty. We can bless the persecutors, praying that God will show them the way to authentic happiness. We must, however, be willing to sacrifice our perquisites or privileges to be God's partners in healing the planet.

CHAPTER NINE

How Can I Keep from Singing?: Life-Giving Death

> Praised be You, my Lord, through our sister Bodily Death,
>   from whom no one can escape...
> How lovely for those who are found in Your
>   Most Holy Will,
> For the second death can do them no harm.
>
> (from the "Canticle of the Creatures")

> "Death has been swallowed up in victory."
> "Where, O death, is your victory?
>   Where, O death, is your sting?"
>
> (1 Corinthians 15:54-55)

While on a recent holiday in Nova Scotia, I attended a brunch at a French bistro on Cape Breton Island. The special guest at the meal was La Mort, identified by a skeletal mask. Death went from table to table leering at the guests as they enjoyed the cuisine. Death took a great interest in me, perhaps because the Grim Reaper intuited my pastoral vocation. Death sat beside me, staring at me, poking me with its cudgel, and laughing at my gallows humor. Death collapsed in hilarity when I quipped, "I guess I'm coming to terms with Death." The event was humorous and I rose to the occasion with several medical and theological one-liners to regale my tablemates and our mysterious intruder. But there was an underlying seriousness. In truth, I will eventually have to come to terms with Death and so will everyone else at the table. We are mortal and our attitudes toward our mortality can add zest to life or plunge us into depression or political and economic behaviors to combat the inevitable.

When I give lectures on death-related topics, I often quip, "Matters of life and death are not relevant to me these days. I'm just entering my midlife crisis provided I live to be 136!" Still, even if I live to be 136, I can't avoid the realities of aging, mortality and the mortality of those I love. This is especially relevant these days as my age and other factors put me at greater risk from the current pandemic. I need the wisdom of Francis and other spiritual leaders to embrace the reality of death while affirming the beauty of life and leaving a legacy of compassion and justice for future generations.

The Reality of Death

In his classic reflection on death and dying, Leo Tolstoy describes Ivan Ilych's struggle to face the reality of his imminent death.

> "Caius is a man, men are mortal, therefore Caius is mortal" had always seemed to him correct as applied to Caius, but by no means to himself. That man Caius meant man in the abstract...and he was not Caius, not an abstract man; he had always been a creature quite, quite distinct from all the others.[35]

Plunged into depression by the reality of his deteriorating health, Ilych moans, "I'll be gone. Where will I be then. Nothing. So where will I be when I'm gone? No, I don't want this!"[36]

Death can deaden our spirits. Thoughts of death can rob life of zest and hopefulness. Facing death can also be an open door to Divinity, inviting us to affirm the sacredness of each moment, recognizing that "this is the day that God has made and I will rejoice and be glad in it" (Psalm 118:24). This precious, passing day brings twenty-four hours for love, beauty, and wonder. This unique moment in time is meant for service to humankind and the good earth. Filled with delight and gratitude for today's unrepeatable opportunities, we can proclaim with the psalmist, "this is the day that the LORD has made, let us rejoice and be glad in it" (Psalm 118:24).

The mortality rate remains 100 percent despite the Western world's medical advances. All of us must come to terms with aging and mortality, even if we live to be 136! But can you imagine writing poetry and singing on your deathbed? Can you imagine affirming the glory of God's world with such gusto that you discover that even Death has a vocation in our relationship with God? Can we celebrate life, singing praises to creation and its Creator, knowing that each breath is a gift and that with our final breath, our journeys continue as part of a never-ending journey in companionship with "Love Divine, All Loves Excelling"?

Facing Death and Finding God

In his final year of his life, Francis's spirit soared as his body failed. Walking was so painful that Francis was forced to ride a donkey. Several months before his death, while on retreat at Alverna, Francis encountered the Living Christ who promised him an unexpected spiritual blessing. At the time, his body was weak from two decades of sacrificial living, the result of following the way of Jesus. Now as he anticipated further physical diminish-ment, Francis became even more committed to walking the path of Jesus in body, mind, and spirit.

It is unlikely that the convalescing Francis expected what would happen next—a vision of Jesus on the Cross followed by the imprinting of his Savior's wounds on Francis's own body. These stigmata invited Francis to see his own wounded body as an avenue of praise and opportunity to share in Christ's suffering love for the world. Francis experienced firsthand God's intimacy in pain as well as celebration. He was reminded that God feels our pain and comforts our fears; he invites us to live in solidarity with all who suffer and use our own personal suffering as a pathway to empathy and compassionate care for all creation.

In the spirit of Psalm 150's affirmation, "let everything that breathes praise God," the physically weary and pain-ridden Francis penned his "Canticle of the Creatures," affirming that all creation and every state of life, from birth to death, reflects God's loving creativity and providence. It is important that we repeat Francis's hymn to locate death as part of God's good creation:

Be praised, my Lord, through all your creatures,
especially through my lord Brother Sun,
who brings the day; and you give light through him.
And he is beautiful and radiant in all his splendor!
Of you, Most High, he bears the likeness.

Praise be You, my Lord, through Sister Moon
and the stars,
in heaven you formed them
clear and precious and beautiful.

Praised be You, my Lord, through Brother Wind,
and through the air, cloudy and serene,
and every kind of weather through which
You give sustenance to Your creatures.
Praised be You, my Lord, through Sister Water,
whichis very useful and humble and precious and chaste.
Praised be You, my Lord, through Brother Fire,
through whom you light the night and he is beautiful
and playful and robust and strong.
Praised be You, my Lord, through Sister Mother Earth,
who sustains us and governs us and who produces
varied fruits with colored flowers and herbs....

Praise and bless my Lord,
and give Him thanks
and serve Him with great humility.[37]

Every moment of creation emerges from God's creative wisdom, and each encounter comes as grace. Every season of our lives is part of a world of praise that awakens us to God's companionship in strength and weakness, comfort and pain, youth and age, living and dying. Our lives in their totality occur within the bounties of nature and the changing of seasons, and this includes the inevitable seasons of aging and death. For those who welcome God in all creation, even death and diminishment can become pathways to experiencing divine blessing.

Life's inevitabilities call us to prayerful contemplation. The necessary losses of our lives, brought about by unavoidable change, can awaken us to God's faithfulness in every season of life. With the author of Lamentations, we can lean on divine providence when we have no strength or courage of our own, trusting that God will make a path where we perceive no way forward.

> The steadfast love of the LORD never ceases,
>   God's mercies never come to an end;
> they are new every morning;
>   great is your faithfulness.
> "The LORD is my portion," says my soul,
>   "therefore I will hope in God."
> (Lamentations 3:22-23, *AP*)

Not long after Francis's mystical vision and experience of the stigmata, the divine imprint on his body, Francis faced his final journey. When a physician friend visited him at Assisi, Francis inquired about his physical condition, prefaced by an affirmation of faith: "Please tell me the truth! For whether I live or die makes no difference to me. My great desire is to do God's will."[38]

Francis's response to the physician's declaration that death was imminent involved lifting his hands to the heavens and calling out as if to a beloved friend, "Welcome, Sister Death!" Then Francis asked his faithful companions Brother Angelo and Brother Leo to chant the "Canticle of the Creatures." As they concluded the canticle, Francis composed another verse:

> Praised by You, my God, through our sister Bodily Death,
> from whom no one can escape.
> How dreadful for those who die in sin,
> How lovely for those who are found in Your Most Holy
>   Will,
> For the second death can do them no harm.

Francis and his companions joyfully sang this stanza throughout the day as a guidepost for Francis's final pilgrimage. The pilgrim who experienced God's companionship in everyday life and the wonders of creation now rejoiced, despite his pain and debilitation, at the next steps of his journey with God. He recognized his solidarity with all who suffer and his constant need for grace, fully aware of the imperfections that badger even those we commend as saints and spiritual leaders.

To some of Francis's companions, the timing of his hymn of praise was unseemly. After all, shouldn't we be serious and mournful at the hour of death, counting our sins and not our blessings? So thought Brother Elias, who challenged Francis's singing as inappropriate for a saint on his deathbed. Though racked with pain, Francis responded, "For in spite of all that I endure, I feel so close to God that I cannot help singing."[39] Francis died with words of praise on his lips. Legend has it that as the saint breathed his last, a flock of larks alighted on the monastery roof and begin chanting in their own hymns of praise, joining their own grief with gratitude for God's presence in Francis's life.

How can we keep from singing? That is life's most challenging question especially in times of trial and tribulation, when the future of our loved ones, ourselves, and the planet is in peril. One evening in mid-September 2008, as I finished leading worship at our congregation in Lancaster, Pennsylvania, I received a call that turned my world upside down. My daughter-in-law, Ingrid, anxiously informed me that our only son, Matt, married just two months, had been admitted to the hospital. Plagued with a recurring cough and chest pressure, he decided to seek treatment at the Georgetown University Hospital emergency room, where he was given x-rays to diagnose the cause. The x-rays revealed a large mass in his chest. When I heard her words, I knew I had to be strong for my family. I reassured her that everything would be all right. But, inside, I also moaned silently, "He's going to die."

The hardest conversation in my life occurred the next morning when I called my wife, who was on a spiritual pilgrimage at Iona, Scotland, to share the news of our son's condition. Speaking the words to Kate made Matt's condition real and filled me with fear for his future.

Two days later, his physician uttered the word we all knew was coming: *cancer*. I felt sorrow and grief at what my son would have to endure, regardless of the outcome. On the outside, as the family's patriarch, I spoke words of hope, but darkness descended on my spirit. So dark that I could not even utter a prayer! The next day as I took my morning walk on the grounds of Georgetown University, a hymn emerged from my desperate sighs too deep for words:

> Lord, have mercy upon me.
> Christ, have mercy upon me.
> Lord, have mercy upon me.

Words failed me. All I could do was tearfully chant these words, reminding me that in times of trial only God's mercy can save us. Grace alone, moving through our lives, the lives of our loved ones, and the planet, is our own only hope for facing the threats we experience and finding the agency and power to confront the evils of our time. "Lord have mercy, Christ have mercy!"

A week later, as the treatments began to provide relief and improvement, I experienced a new song bursting forth, filling me with grateful hope. I knew that Matt's journey would be long and that the treatments would be difficult, but God gave me a vision of a hopeful future, wrapped in a song from my Baptist childhood, guiding my pathway forward and giving me strength and wisdom for my uncertain pilgrimage as parent and husband. I was moved to sing of my Baptist youth, "Great Is Thy Faithfulness," giving thanks for God's faithfulness and the mercies are new with each morning.

Like the dying saint, I discovered that Matt's and my lives were part of a larger story, an unending and open-ended adventure, grounded in God's creative and loving wisdom that brought forth galaxies, gave birth to our planet, brought forth wise women and men, prophets and sages, and in the fullness of time, Jesus of Nazareth, the healer and savior. My life and Matt's emerged from God's love, and whatever would occur in the future, we would always be embraced by God's unending and irresistible love. The hymn gave me courage and confidence that in life and death, "all I have needed God's hand has provided, great is God's faithfulness unto me." Filled with a new song that God had bestowed upon me, I could go on, trusting God with the uncertain future, summoning the strength I needed to fulfill my vocation as parent, husband, pastor, and professor, knowing God to be the air I breathe and the energy that enlivens. With the prophet Jeremiah, who heard God's promise in a time of national calamity, I could live faithfully and act decisively trusting God's promise: "For surely I know the plans I have for you, says the LORD, plans for your welfare and not for harm, to give you a future with hope" (Jeremiah 29:11).

Now, over a decade later, two lively young boys greet me most afternoons. Miracle children, my son's boys, my grandchildren, revealing God's faithfulness and calling me to be faithful as God's companion in healing the earth, so that they might also have a future with great hope.

Our hopeful melodies are not opiates deadening the spirits of the masses, turning us heavenward in escape from life's injustices. Our hymns of praise embrace life's challenges and summon us to bring God's realm "on earth as it is in heaven." They are talismans that deliver us from weak resignation to the evils of our time and empower us to say yes to justice, hospitality, healing, and planetary well-being. With songs of praise in our heart, we can chase away the darkness of hopelessness and discover eternity in our quest to heal the earth. No demagogue, tyrant, or oppressor can silence our hymns of joyful praise. In chanting our hymns, we experience, as Francis did, God's providential care in the maelstrom of public life and national crisis, as well as in the privacy of our living and dying.

Inspired by God's compassionate presence, fear is transformed to courage and despair gives way to hope, whether in our personal lives or the political area. We can intone Robert Lowry's hymn of gratitude and hope for all life's seasons:

> Thro' all the tumult and the strife
> I hear the music ringing;
> It finds an echo in my soul—
> How can I keep from singing?

Ninety years after it was first written, Doris Plenn added a stanza to reflect the divisive politics of the 1950s McCarthy era, a time in which innocent people were brought before congressional tribunals as a result of their political affiliations. As we face our own time of personal and political uncertainty, we can also discover that God is with us, sustaining our spirits, ensuring our integrity, and giving us wisdom to confront the powers of darkness.

> When tyrants tremble, sick with fear,
>> And hear their death-knell ringing,
> When friends rejoice both far and near,
>> How can I keep from singing?

With the saint of Assisi, we can claim our place in of God's great hymn of creation and reconciliation. God chants within us and with us, bringing glory, gratitude, and praise in times of social and political upheaval and giving us more than we ask or imagine in response to life's challenges with grace and determination. God's melody of love accompanies us in the darkest valley. God's hymn of creation will outlive every demagogue, tyrant, and oppressor.

With a song in our hearts, death and diminishment cannot thwart our commitment to embody God's vision of shalom and healing. Founding mother of the Catholic Worker Movement in North America, Dorothy Day lived by the spirit of gratitude, hope, and empowerment throughout her adult life, picketing and praying, and providing food for the hungry and hope for the marginalized. In her seventies, sidelined by health issues and no longer able to run the *Catholic Worker* newspaper or travel to protest injustice, she confessed that "my job now is prayer."[40] In the spirit of St. Francis, Dorothy Day knew that our prayers and chants provide a pathway toward new horizons of justice and call us to keep the faith, despite the machinations of the powerful and our own debilitation.

God's way inspires and sustains us and gives us courage to face

Death in all its masks, whether personal, social, or political. As improbable as it may seem, in our world of praise we can welcome Sister Death with song, greet the morning news with hope, and face the impossible with dreams of everlasting life! God is here with the vision of shalom, inspiring us to be instruments of peace and creative transformation.

IN THE SPIRIT OF ST. FRANCIS

In the wake of the destruction of Jerusalem and the Babylonian exile, Judean bards composed hymns of lamentation. The world the world they knew and loved was gone forever. Would another world emerge of the rubble of their lives? Would their spirits ever be restored?

> By the rivers of Babylon—
>   there we sat down and there we wept
>   when we remembered Zion
> ...
> How could we sing the LORD's song
>   in a foreign land?
> (Psalm 137:1, 4)

The singers' despair turned to rage and prayers for the destruction of the children of their captors (see Psalm 137:8-9). But rage was not the final word. Tragedy gave way to praise. The power of the psalms is their recognition of the totality of human experience, from exaltation and wonder to despair and anger. Yet the psalmist places all these emotions in God's hands, recognizing the transforming power of divine companionship, regardless of our current spiritual or emotional state.

Search me, O God, and know my heart;
   test me and know my thoughts.
See if there is any wicked way in me,
   and lead me in the way everlasting.
(Psalm 139:23-24)

In taking every experience to God in prayer, words of praise burst forth even in direst of circumstances. We receive a new song and join in a chorus of praise in which all creation and ourselves praise God (see Psalm 150:6).

Francis was no stranger to pain and debilitation. In his mid-forties, Francis was struck down with chronic illness and physical diminishment. Yet, during this time of disability, words of gratitude and praise welled up in response to God's glory revealed in all creation, including the dying process. In the spirit of Dag Hammarskjöld's prayer, cited earlier:

For all that has been—thanks!
For all that shall be—yes!

Can we sing God's song in the world of illness and disability? Can we sing hymns of gratitude in an era of climate change and pandemic? Can we sing praises as we face the reality of death? As we embody the spirit of St. Francis, I invite you to share in the following spiritual practices.

Living with St. Francis's Canticle
In the days ahead, read the following sections of the "Canticle" each morning and evening. Begin your time of prayerful reflection with a moment of silence, followed by gratitude for the new day

and, in the evening, gratitude for the gifts of today. Then, silently read this selection from Francis's "Canticle" twice with a pause between readings.

> Praised be You, my Lord,
> through those who give pardon for Your love,
> and bear infirmity and tribulation.
> Blessed are those who endure in peace
> for by You, Most High, they shall be crowned.
> Praised be You, my Lord,
> through our Sister Bodily Death,
> from whom no living man can escape...
> Blessed are those whom death will
> find in Your most holy will,
> for the second death shall do them no harm.
> Praise and bless my Lord,
> and give Him thanks
> and serve Him with great humility.

Notice any insights that emerge from your prayerful encounter with the "Canticle." Conclude with a prayer of thanksgiving for the gifts of life and for insight in embodying your prayers in daily life. Let this prayer be a talisman enabling you to faithfully face your fears with God as your companion.

The Great Thanksgiving

German mystic Meister John Eckhart counseled that if the only prayer you can make is "thank you," that will suffice. In an inter-dependent, God-filled universe, we can give thanks for God's companionship in sickness and death. Life's limitations can be the source of new possibilities and an opportunity to witness to our faith. As Viktor Frankl notes in his recollection of life in the German concentration camps, we are challenged to be worthy of our suffering. Misfortune and pain don't excuse us from living up to our moral and spiritual obligations.

In the spirit of Francis's affirmation of Death as a window into everlasting life, contemplate your current circumstances, noting your limitations and challenges as well as achievements and joys. Looking at your life in its totality, for what are you thankful? What negative experiences or misfortunes turned out to be opportunities for grace? What divine graces are you currently experiencing in the limitations of your life? Recognizing that in all things God is working for good, where do you see divine providence operating in your life right now? In what ways do you feel inspired to praise God despite your limitations and challenges? Praise recognizes the harsh realities of life and places them in the context of God's loving companionship and the quest for healing and justice. Conclude your reflections with prayers for God's presence as you look toward this life's final adventure.

Prayers of gratitude amid life's personal and political challenges do not deny the realities of pain and suffering. They place the challenges of our lives in a larger perspective, enabling us to experience God's care in all things, and empowering us to confront the many faces of death with courage and hope.

Songs of Praise
Music can transform the human spirit. In the depths of uncertainty for my son's life, a song of hope and gratitude flowed into my heart. I couldn't make it alone. I had to trust everything to

God's grace. The *Kyrie* and the hymn "Great Is Thy Faithfulness" were my companions in the dark night of parenting.

With a song in our hearts, we can face death threats and the machinations of the powers of evil. At the height of the Civil Rights movement, freedom marchers sang "We Shall Overcome" to calm their fears and give them courage and hope, knowing that the moral arc of the universe bends toward justice. These words can inspire us as we face the reality of death.

> We are not afraid,
> We are not afraid,
> We are not afraid, today.
> Oh, deep in my heart,
> I do believe
> We shall overcome someday.

In this spiritual exercise, consider your hymns or melodies of faith, whether narrowly spiritual or broadly secular. God's wisdom speaks through every nurturing song. What songs or hymns, sacred or secular, deepen your faith? What songs or hymns strengthen your spirit and enable you to face debilitation and death? Take time to sing these songs prayerfully, trusting with Francis that, in every circumstance, God will make a way where there is no way, and that God will be our companion each moment in living, dying, and beyond.

The Great Yes!
In the animated film *Toy Story*, Buzz Lightyear shouts "To infinity and beyond" to give heart to his companions and himself. As he faced death, Francis embraced God's great yes. Death is not the

termination of life's possibilities but the beginning of a new adventure in companionship with the One who walks with us each step of the way. We can sing praises to God's presence in death because God is the faithful wellspring of possibility and adventure.

In this spiritual practice, reflect on your great yes. What is your great yes? What gives you hope as you face aging? What gives you persistence and integrity as you confront the apparently unsolvable problems of climate change, injustice, immigration and migration, and polarization? What is the great yes that sustains you as you face the great unknown of death? Can you face the great mystery with hope and trust that God is with you and that nothing can separate you from the love of God in Christ Jesus? (see Romans 8:38-39)

Spirituality inspires dreams and visions, imagination and visualization. Take some time to imagine your destiny beyond the grave, visualizing the contours of the afterlife, your companions, your new adventures, your relationship with God and Christ. Take time to place, as Francis did, the totality of your living and dying in God's care, knowing that God has a vision for you, a future filled with hope, and nothing in all creation can separate you from God's embracing love. Make a commitment to bring your heavenly vision to everyday life with acts of kindness and a commitment to justice, knowing that whether we live or die we are in God's loving arms. With the troubadour of Assisi, how can we keep from singing?

1. Francis of Assisi, *Francis of Assisi: Early Documents, Volume One* (New York: New City Press, 1999), 40.
2. Dorothy Day, *Selected Writings,* edited by Robert Ellsberg (Maryknoll, NY: Orbis Books, 2017), xi.
3. Day, xi.
4. Day, 51.
5. Andre Vauchez, *Francis of Assisi: The Life and Afterlife of a Medieval Saint* (New Haven: Yale University Press, 2016), 22.
6. Dag Hammarsjold, *Markings (*New York: Knopf, 1964), 89.
7. Thomas of Celano, "The First Life of St. Francis," in Martin Habig, *St. Francis of Assisi: Omnibus of Sources* (Cincinnati: Franciscan Media, 2010), 318.
8. Phyllis Tickle, *The Great Emergence: How Christianity is Changing and Why* (Grand Rapids: Baker, 2008), 8.
9. Clare of Assisi, *Clare of Assisi, The Early Documents,* edited by Regis J. Armstrong (New York: New City Press, 2006), 51.
10. Pope Francis, *Praised be to You—Laudato Si!: On Care for Our Common Home* (San Francisco: Ignatius Press, 2015), 7 .
11. Murray Bodo, *Francis: The Journey and the Dream* (Cincinnati: Franciscan Media, 2011), 169-170.
12. Francis of Assisi, *Francis of Assisi: The Saint—The Early Documents,* 234.
13. *Francis of Assisi: The Saint—The Early Documents,* 235.
14. *Francis of Assisi: The Saint—The Early Documents,* 250.
15. *Francis of Assisi: The Saint—The Early Documents,* 251.
16. https://www.washingtonpost.com/religion/2019/09/18/progressive-seminary-students-offered-confession-plants-what-are-we-make-it/
17. Howard Thurman, *With Heart and Mind* (New York: Harcourt Brace and Company, 1979), 12.
18. Alfred North Whitehead, *Process and Reality: Corrected Edition* (New York: Free Press, 1979), 351.
19. Arthur Miller, *Death of a Salesman* (New York: Penguin Books, 1976), 56.
20. Murray Bodo, *Francis: The Journey and the Dream* (Cincinnati: Franciscan Media, 2011) 169-170.

21. Francis of Assisi, *Francis—The Saint: The Early Documents* (New York: New City Press, 1999), 201-202.

22. Francis and Clare of Assisi, *Francis and Clare: The Complete Works* (Mahwah, NJ: Paulist Press, 1982), 192.

23. Leonardo Boff, *Francis of Assisi: A Model for Human Liberation* (Maryknoll: Orbis Books, 2006), 64.

24. Francis of Assisi and Clare of Assisi, *Francis and Clare: The Complete Works*, 197.

25. Marco Bartoli, *Saint Clare: Beyond the Legend* (Cincinnati: Franciscan Media, 2010), 26.

26. Bartoli, 95.

27. Dag Hammarskjold, Markings (New York: Alfred A. Knopf, 1964), 89.

28. Thomas Merton, *Conjectures of a Guilty Bystander* (New York: Doubleday, 1966), 156. (Quoted in Thomas Merton, *Thomas Merton: Essential Writings,* edited by Christine M. Bochen (Maryknoll, NY: Orbis Books, 2000), 90.

29. Martin Luther King, Jr., *Testament of Hope: The Essential Writings and Speeches of Martin Luther King, Jr.* (edited by James M. Washington), (New York: HarperSanFrancisco, 1986), 208.

30. Alfred North Whitehead, *Religion in the Making* (Cambridge: Cambridge University Press, 2011), 40.

31. Alfred North Whitehead, *Adventures in Ideas* (New York: Free Press, 1961), 285.

32. Francis of Assisi, *Francis of Assisi—The Saint: Early Documents* (New York: New City Press, 1990), 240.

33. Harold Koenig, *The Healing Power of Faith* (New York: Simon and Schuster, 2001); Dale Matthews, *The Faith Factor: Proof of the Healing Power of Prayer* (New York: Penguin, 1999); Larry Dossey, *Healing Words: The Power of Prayer and the Practice of Medicine* (San Francisco: Harper One, 1995); Larry Dossey, *Prayer Is Good Medicine* (New York: HarperSan Francisco, 1997).

34. Bruce Epperly, *The Energy of Love: Reiki and Christian Healing* (Gonzales, FL: Energion Publications, 2017) and Bruce Epperly and Katherine Epperly, *Reiki Healing Touch and the Way of Jesus* (Kelowna, BC: Northstone Books, 2005). Also, Bruce Epperly, *Healing Marks: Healing and Spirituality in Mark's Gospel* (Gonzales, FL: Energion Publications, 2012) and *God's Touch: Faith, Wholeness,*

and the Healing Miracles of Jesus (Louisville: Westminster/John Knox, 2001).

35. Leo Tolstoy, *The Death of Ivan Ilych* (New York: Bantam Books, 1987), 93.

36. Tolstoy, 89.

37. Murray Bodo, *Francis: The Journey and the Dream* (Cincinnati, OH: Franciscan Media, 2011), 169-170.

38. Omer Englebert, *St. Francis of Assisi: A Biography* (Cincinnati: Franciscan Media, 2013), 310.

39. Englebert, 311.

40. Dorothy Day, *Selected Writings,* (Maryknoll, NY: Orbis Books, 2005), *xl.*

Franciscan Media is a nonprofit ministry of the Franciscan Friars of St. John the Baptist Province. Through the publication of spiritual books, *St. Anthony Messenger* magazine, and online media properties such as *Saint of the Day, Minute Meditations,* and *Faith & Family,* Franciscan Media seeks to share God's love in the spirit of St. Francis of Assisi. For more information, to support us, and to purchase our products, visit franciscanmedia.org.

ABOUT THE AUTHOR

Rev. Dr. Bruce G. Epperly has served as a congregational pastor, university chaplain, professor, and seminary administrator for over forty years. He is currently Senior Pastor of South Congregational Church, United Church of Christ, Centerville, Massachusetts. He is the author of more than fifty books on practical theology, ministry, and spirituality, healing and wholeness, and process theology, including *The Mystic in You: Discovering a God-filled World*, the award-winning *Tending to the Holy: The Practice of the Presence of God in Ministry*, and *Mystics in Action: Twelve Saints for Today*. He lives on Cape Cod, Massachusetts, with his wife Rev. Dr. Katherine Gould Epperly, his son, daughter-in-law, and grandchildren.